EXPLORING
THE
CHRISTIAN WORLD MIND

EXPLORING
THE
CHRISTIAN WORLD MIND

PERSONAL INTERVIEWS — THE UNITED NATIONS COMMUNITY

DAVID WESLEY SOPER

PHILOSOPHICAL LIBRARY

New York

Printed in the United States of America

CONTENTS

APOLOGIA PRO VITA SUA

These chapters were completed with specific and extended footnotes, identifying each and every author, source, publisher, edition and page with elaborate detail. The quotes are therefore genuine and authentic. Footnotes, in my experience, are of primary interest to scholars, often for economic reasons buried alive in free libraries, rather than to book-buying laymen.

The cause of the chapel basement fire, attributed to a troubled youth, is as yet unknown, but when it was extinguished several volumes quoted here and stored there, with a number of other manuscripts, of classroom and Manhattan's Keedick Lecture Bureau presentations, in frequent use about the nation, were destroyed — together with a two-inch end of this manuscript in early form projecting from a shelf, the part containing all the footnotes, with no duplicate copies in existence.

The first idea was simply to throw the work away, shed a tear, and proceed with other commitments. Careful re-reading of what remained, however, suggested the intrinsic value, and the possibility of careful re-editing and re-typing, with the addition of further scheduled interviews. To this we, the office and I, directed our immediate attention.

The point of the entire series is, of course, a simple one — an urgent recommendation that sensitive folk, on both sides of the White Curtain now separating the three Protestants and the one Roman in every four Christians (themselves, according to the New Delhi World Council of Churches, one third the Earth's present population — 900 million in 2 billion 700 million — Christ's creative minority, his salt, his light, his leaven in the loaf), now laboring to advance the Free World Mind, carry forward in parliamentary manner, not unlike that of the United Nations Organization, their mutual respect and acceptance, in obedience to Christ's prayer, "That they all may be one; as thou, Father, art in me, and I in thee, that they also may be one in us; that the world may believe that thou hast sent me . . . that they may be one, even as we are one: I in them, and thou in me, that they may be made perfect in one; and that the world may know that thou hast sent me, and hast loved them, as thou hast loved me." (John 17:21-23 King James Version)

David Wesley Soper

FOREWORD

The purpose in the following pages is to report, and interpret, informally, the thinking of a selection of contemporary minds (in Christian countries), as they contemplate the remainder of the Twentieth Century. It is evident that an essential Free World mentality exists with wide diversity.

My friends the Romans insist upon the Thomist three-story house of Science, Philosophy, and Theology; I agree. My friends the Barthians insist that we include God in Christianity; I agree. My friends the disciples of Dodd insist that Revelation is a dialogue, not a lecture; I agree. Oxnam has insisted that Protestantism is religious freedom, that Romanism limits liberty. I see his point. But I refuse to give up any of my friends. We Protestants need not less freedom but more faith. I refuse to give up Barth. I see no reason why a place for God cannot be found in western thought; we have room for everything else. I find Dodd's emphasis upon the reality of man basic in all mental, moral, social and political traffic. Can no place for the dignity of man be found in the Free World?

Diversity accompanying unity, difference within fellowship — Romanism and Protestantism, Greek Orthodox and Anglican, within the authentically catholic, and Catholic, World Council of Churches — is sound health; it is the sane recognition that no man or movement is sufficient alone.

Each special theological position within the Church of Christ rightly emphasizes a truth otherwise underaccented. Someone has to beat the drum for every aspect of value. If any one mind could comprehend the whole of Christianity, for example, Christianity would have been a small invention. To say that one theology and not another may be heard is to underestimate the meaning of fellowship. For centuries the Church has woven into the fabric of faith many necessary threads. The atheist thread, in the main, has been rejected, though the atheist refusal of infinitesimal substitutes for the infinite Reality has been accepted, and insisted upon; the thread of human self-sufficiency has been rejected — the Universe upholds man, not man the Universe; the thread of the denial of Christ, the denial of incarnate moral love, has been rejected. But within the One Fold, under the One Shepherd, difference means Fellowship, Fellowship means Freedom — and the Time for uniting Faithfulness is Now!

The interviews are arranged, in the following pages, not in the secondary sequence of time, rather in the primary sequence of interest.

I wish to express my profound indebtedness to each intellectual leader for his generosity in time and thought, and to the following magazines and journals, in which the chapters indicated first appeared, for permission to reprint: (CHRISTENDOM, *An Interview With Jacques Maritain;* CHRISTIAN CENTURY, *As Catholics See Us;* ZION'S HERALD, *G. K. Chesterton and Dorothy Collins, W. A. Visser 'T Hooft, Disunion At Amsterdam, Christolph Barth, Emil Brunner, C. S. Lewis, T. S. Eliot, Arnold J. Toynbee, William R. Inge, Nathaniel Micklem, Newton Flew, Reinhold Niebuhr;* THE CONGREGATIONAL MINISTERS' QUARTERLY, *Charles H. Dodd;* WORLD OUTLOOK, *T. W. E. Sommer;* WORKERS WITH YOUTH, *Donald O. Soper;* DREW GATEWAY, *Nicholas Berdiaeff*).

David Wesley Soper

EXPLORING
THE
CHRISTIAN WORLD MIND

KARL BARTH'S POINT OF VIEW

It was my privilege to dine with Karl Barth, and his friend of twenty years, Pierre Maury, Paris Protestant pastor, but two hours after the delivery of one of the Neo-Reformation Leader's more provocative addresses.

I indicated that less was known in America about his personal biography than about his theocentric theology. He reminded me of an article, *How My Mind Has Changed,* he had written for THE CHRISTIAN CENTURY, to which he has since appended a sequel. The point, he stressed, was simple enough. Smiling, he added: "I have never had a Damascus Road experience; I have never been converted." He had been trained for the ministry in the mentality of Ritschl and Harnack, and thus equipped as he put it, "Without a Gospel," had gone forth to serve for ten years as a country pastor. During this period he had discovered that he had nothing worth their trouble to give the people, nothing for them to live by, nothing for them to trust in. Through much searching of soul he had realized his own shallow inadequacy, had rediscovered the insufficiency of man and the sufficiency of God.

I explained that I had made a similar pilgrimage, proceeding from ten years of atheism into faith. I related also, to his amusement, the story of my friend, Will-Mathis Dunn, who had gone from a southern seminary into the Texas oil fields to preach. He had given his congregation all that he had received, had informed them at length concerning the J E D and P sources woven together to form the fabric of the Pentateuch. He had then told his patient flock about the P D E and J sources, by way of variation. Then, having run out of material, he had made up his mind to acquire a Gospel worth preaching. He had proceeded forthwith to five years of graduate study with Edwin Lewis and Lynn Harold Hough at Drew University, where he had heard the Voice of God in the voices of men.

1

We spoke of Barth's son, Christoph, with whom I was later to share a pleasant period at Barth's home in Basle. Christoph was engaged, said his father, in a missionary career in Dutch Borneo, teaching a native language as well as the Gospel. His book on the Old Testament, then not yet issued in English, had gained wide recognition on the continent, and was, said Barth, a top quality work.

At Karl Barth's request, I described briefly American Methodism, and, in particular, the good work of Bishop G. Bromley Oxnam, of whom he had not heard. I cited the conclusion of a LIFE Magazine article, which had stated that Methodism, like America, "was weak on theology and strong on action." I described, to Barth's amusement, the squirming of a well-known American Churchman during his afternoon address. I stressed the obvious fact that true faith and worthy zeal did abound in American Methodism, but suggested that not without cause had it been said that Methodism had substituted a Crusade for Prohibition and Pacifism for the preaching of the Gospel, a superficial prudery for spiritual freedom, activism and machinery for intellectual and spiritual exertion. Pierre Maury felt that I was a bit too severe in my characterization. Barth indicated that his understanding of American Protestantism, in general, was identical with mine.

At this point Roy L. Smith, then editor of THE CHRISTIAN ADVOCATE, America's Methodist Weekly, stopped at our table and introduced himself.

I urged that Barth come over into our American Macedonia and help us — which he has since done, and we rejoiced in his presence at the University of Chicago — Spring 1962. He said that he had received innumerable invitations, but that Dr. Adolph Keller of Geneva had told him about American speaking tours, all machine-gun efficiency with addresses every few minutes and endless train travel, and he had decided to remain in Switzerland.

Barth asserted that some unbelief was present at the Amsterdam World Assembly, from Switzerland as well as from America, but that the endeavor, spoken or unspoken, to reduce the World Council's Christology would come to nought.

2

I quoted Brunner's characterization of the difference between their two theologies, which the Sage of Zurich had given me at his home. "Barth thinks as a Churchman, and I think as a Missionary. Barth speaks as though his hearers understood a Biblical and theological vocabulary; I speak as though my hearers were pagans." Barth was deeply amused, and retorted: "I suppose that is one of his profound observations!" I explained further that Brunner had said to me: "I imagine from America Barth and I look a good deal alike." To which I had replied: "Yes, in America you both are suspected of believing in God." Barth considered this an excellent answer.

I referred to Brunner's accusation that Barth had not attacked Communist totalitarianism, whereas he had attacked Nazi totalitarianism with sustained vigor. Barth replied: "Brunner saw fit to attack me in an open letter on this theme. I simply do not feel about Communism as I did about Nazism, though I heartily disapprove of coercive collectivism. I am very suspicious of the Mammon-worship deeply embedded in your American Capitalism, where true freedom exists almost, though not quite, as rarely as in Russia. I confess I would rather be forced to live in America than in Russia. American Christians, I think, have been insufficiently critical of the private ownership of property, land, capital, etc." I remembered that Barth had normally voted the Socialist ticket in Basle, though he had never approved the Mammon-worship of Marxian materialism.

I was convinced, as we talked, that Barth was basically sympathetic both to Western freedom and to Eastern economics, that he was therefore of one mind with the English endeavor to find a working compromise between the brotherhood without freedom of the East and the freedom without brotherhood of the West.

I felt, as I left Barth and his friend, after the evening filled with light, yet filled also with laughter, that a high point for me had been reached. Barth, whom I regard with affection, whom I respect as a contemporary prophet, in whose voice may be heard an authentic *Vox Dei*, so clearly possessed the joy and simplicity, the spiritual freedom and guileless trust, of a child.

THE ROMAN POINT OF VIEW

JACQUES MARITAIN

It was not easy for M. Maritain to arrange to see me, for his mornings were devoted to research and writing, whence have come his distinguished contributions. His evenings were occupied with crowded appointments. Calls upon the then French Ambassador to the Vatican were numerous. Nonetheless, with the assistance of the enchanting secretary, Mlle. Sylvain, the interview was set for four-fifteen.

A drawing room was selected for our conversation in Rome's Palazzo Taverna, and an obsequious butler placed me in comfort beside a great vase of flowers. A moment later His Excellency, M. Jacques Maritain, entered, took my hand cordially, and seated himself at my side. With the kindliest grace he considered and answered my queries. He expressed his pleasure that our mutual friend, Nicholas Berdiaeff, had urged me to visit him.

I had prepared my spirit for the interview by spending a while at the Vatican, where, through the advocacy of my friend, Don Carlo Carbone, Roman priest and professor of religious art, I was received with other pilgrims by His Holiness, Pope Pius XII. I confess that I was deeply moved as I gazed upon the spare figure and kindly face of Peter's direct successor. The ecstatic shouts of the pilgrims increased my emotion. The Pope gave us his blessing, directed bliss also to our families, urged that we take our problems directly to God in prayer. I was reminded, during the delivery of these good words, of a Roman friend who once said to me: "I believe in praying to the saints, but I have so little time for daily devotions that, when I pray, I take my petitions straight to Headquarters."

The mediaeval and heraldic colour of the Vatican, its magnificence in structure and beauty, and the unequalled glory of its artistic masterpieces, constitute an incomparable monument to the Faith of Augustine, Francis, Thomas, and Dante. Outside the Vatican, and in striking contrast to the prodigal splendour of Rome's ancient ruins, was the appalling poverty of the people. I was impressed too that Rome's innumerable billboards seemed devoted exclusively to the advertisement of quick "V. D." cures. Sorokin's principle of polarization — glory and shame existing side by side — was clearly illustrated; Vatican and venereal disease, the one seeking to redeem man's spirit, the other seeking to destroy his flesh, competed for attention; there the Roman Church and the International Black Market had their rival headquarters.

M. Maritain had long fascinated me, for his name had been often mentioned at Lynn Harold Hough's Graduate Seminar at Drew University. In pursuing my own later studies I had frequently consulted his penetrating volumes, Roman in idea, broadly Catholic in spirit.

On many occasions the apparently irreconcilable philosophies of Thomas Aquinas and Kierkegaard had evoked in me a keen desire to find a basis for reconciliation. At once therefore I asked whether these two thought structures, the one characteristic of Romanism, the other of Protestantism, might not be harmonized. M. Maritain immediately declared that, in his estimation, Kierkegaard was not a philosopher but a hero of faith, a true mystic. There was no sufficient reason to consider the opposed positions irreconcilable. Between Thomism and the Existentialism of Heidegger and Sartre there was an unbridgeable chasm, for Thomism could not peacefully be wedded to irrationalism. Yet between the Existentialism of Kierkegaard and Gabrielle Marcel and the philosophy of Thomas there was much common ground.

Jacques Maritain mentioned that a new book of his was then in process of publication in France dealing precisely with what he regarded as a strong element of Existentialism in Thomas Aquinas. It was assumed by various writers that the Scholasticism of Thomas had been focused, in true Greek fashion, not upon existence but upon essence. After careful research M. Maritain had come to the conclusion, unlike Gilson, that this popular assumption was false. The mentality of Thomas had been a preoccupation with the problems of existing individuals. It had been existence, not essence, with which Thomas had been primarily concerned. Hence, the basis for reconciliation between Thomism and Existentialism already existed in the former.

We might have pressed the question further. In particular I would have asked concerning the specific divergence between the two conceptions of living Christianity. Thomism appeared preoccupied with the objective, Kierkegaard with the subjective Church. In one the structure of Christian thought and faith was *there,* so to speak, for anyone to take or leave. In the other only the subjective crisis of faith, the passion of personal consecration, was significant. Was the Church to be considered *outside* or *inside* the believer — or both, and which primarily? It was not possible to pursue this topic further, for I had promised Mlle. Sylvain that I would not trespass upon later appointments previously scheduled. Had this discussion been extended, I imagine that the Kierkegaardian subjectivity would, in M. Maritain's opinion, have been classified as the Thomist doctrine of personal discipleship, merely one idea in the total cluster of Christian Truths. The essential priority of Roman objectivity would probably have prevailed. However, M. Maritain must in no way be held responsible for this projection of my own imagination. His conclusion might have been that Kierkegaardian subjectivism had been the rediscovery of Roman personal experience.

It is to be recognized that in M. Maritain's rejection of the Existentialism of Heidegger and Sartre as "irrational," the standpoint of rationalism was, by inference, assumed. With a pure rationalism is not Kierkegaardian Existentialism equally at war? It is possible that the problem is unsolvable, since the fundamental presuppositions of the two philosophies are so distinct. Perhaps Protestantism must be forever freedom, subjectivism, or lose one reason for separate existence from Rome. It must be borne in mind, however, that subjectivism is by no means the whole of Protestantism, for classical Protestantism had also an objective Faith, the Biblical testimony to Christ as God and Saviour, and an objective Church, governed not by papal decree but by parliamentary agreement.

6

As the second subject for discussion I quoted Arnold J. Toynbee's assertion, emphasized in the second three of his many volume *Study of History*, that Christendom might still be a unity, and the deification of parochial sovereign States have been avoided, had the Popes of the fifteenth and sixteenth centuries accepted the parliamentary limitation upon their absolute authority offered by the Conciliar Movement. M. Maritain had not heard the Toynbee statement, and gave it some consideration. From the viewpoint of an historian, he said, the assertion in question was undoubtedly true. However, Toynbee had failed to take into account the nature of the Roman Church, viewed from within. Only recently the Pope had characterized civil government as legitimately receiving its authority from men, whereas the government of the Church had received its authority from God. The two kinds of government were basically distinct; no proper analogy could be drawn between them. The root difficulty in the fifteenth and subsequent centuries had been the erroneous belief of the mediaeval dynasties that they ruled by Divine Right. The fact was otherwise, for the monarchs had in no case received their authority from God; they had rather seized it by force out of the hands of the people. The Pope, as the Representative of Christ, had not received his authority from men. He had not been at liberty to bestow his power upon an ecclesiastical Parliament. To a limited degree, the parliamentary principle existed in practice within the Roman Church in the Pope's appointed College of Cardinals, a kind of President's Cabinet.

From this pointed summary of a characteristic Roman position, our discussion led to a related problem. Exactly what was necessary for the re-union of Christendom? Evangelical Protestants, by virtue of their faith in Christ as God and Saviour, recognized a basic common ground with Rome; at times these Christians felt themselves isolated in a vast throng of doubting Thomases. Among leaders, I stated, the idea had been advanced that Protestant denominations, Unitarians not excluded, might be received into parliamentary Fellowship, acknowledging the Pope as the Symbol of Roman authoritarian unity, but permitted, like the Franciscans, the Dominicans, and the Jesuits, to retain their own Regula and their characteristic emphases in faith. M. Maritain replied that

7

the reunion of Christendom could materialize only on the basis of agreement — first, on the essentials of the Creed, second, on the authority of the Pope to decide disputed issues of faith and order. If the Pope relinquished his absolute power and became merely Christendom's permanent Presiding Officer, Rome would no longer be Rome, and the Christian Faith itself might conceivably be voted out of existence by a parliamentary majority.

I wrote these paragraphs, in first draft, at the Basilica of San Paolo on the Ostian Road south of Rome. Near the spot St. Paul was beheaded; under the high altar of the Great Church, it is believed, his body lies buried. It is significant that St. Paul received his call, his gospel, and his authority, on the Damascus Road, directly from Christ, not from St. Peter — in the view of the author of the *Acts of the Apostles,* probably Luke, and in his own emphasis on the primacy of personal justifying faith. He began and ended his great ministry "outside Rome." Verily if Romanism is the Church of St. Peter, Protestantism, it would seem, is the Church of St. Paul. And, as a matter of history, did not St. Paul make a considerable contribution to Roman theology?

We came at last to the topic of major immediate interest. It might seem at first that the question of Protestant resurrection ought to be asked only of non-Romans, but a Voice is always needed from an external perspective. M. Maritain believed, he said, that two outstanding needs existed in contemporary Protestantism, one a recovery of what the Quakers called "The Inner Light" — prayer and faith and devotion of an exalted kind, true Life within — the other an escape from this generation's all-embracing, and all-dissolving, pseudo-social gospel, through an intellectual revival. America's Drew University, in particular, M. Maritain asserted, offered an excellent example of the necessary intellectual renaissance, a reaction against sentimentality. A conscious companionship with God, which, as a matter of history, was a central emphasis in classical Protestantism, and the intellectual seriousness of the Great Reformers — these were the definitive Protestant necessities.

W. A. Visser 'T Hooft's emphasis upon a return to original Protestantism is similar, though distinct in its ascription of final

8

authority to the Word of God rather than the interpreting Church. Similar also is the demand from Emil Brunner that "a live theology" be recovered.

At length we came to practical politics. Exactly how far to the political left might a man go who found himself at the theological right? There was no identity whatever, asserted Maritain, between a theological and a political right. He had stressed in all his writings, particularly in the volume, *True Humanism*, which he recommended as the strongest presentation of his ethical and political philosophy, that classical Christianity was neutral about political mechanics; it simply required responsible solutions to social problems. His position in matters political, he acknowledged, was virtually identical with that of Reinhold Niebuhr and Nicholas Berdiaeff. Christianity required group mobilization of resources and energies to meet group needs. Totalitarianism's coercive Collectivism annihilated the spirit and the identity of the individual, ruled by irresponsible caprice, proved a government of brigands. Laissez-faire Anarchy, however, turned of necessity into a regime of force and fraud, of violence and hypocrisy. The Christian Community, on the other hand, rallied the human and the mechanical best for a common assault against common obstacles to social and personal well-being.

Because Protestantism in the main, he said, had regarded the political world as beyond the claim of the Gospel, it had allowed the State to become secular. The ensuing moral anarchy had brought forth many things, but little notably based on Christian charity. Christianity, to obey its Lord, to express its true nature, had to move back into the political world, claiming all for Christ, demanding the execution of the Divine will in Society as in the Church and the Soul.

ETIENNE GILSON

At M. Gilson's home in Paris a kindly woman in middle age led me to a handsome living room. Presently a young man of nineteen appeared and explained that his father had gone to the Senat, where I would be sure to find him. It was not known whether he would dine at home.

I asked the son if I might interview him. After several protestations of inability to shed light on difficult problems, he consented. He spoke very acceptable English, and proved as stimulating of mind as he was handsome in appearance. He had begun his first year at the Sorbonne, where he had enrolled in standard Liberal Arts courses. He hoped eventually to specialize in philosophy, his father's field. Among his teachers was M. Jean Wall, whose interest in Kierkegaard had been described to me by Madame Gabrielle Marcel, during a breakfast conversation at Madame Chessex' in the French Swiss Alps.

The name of the younger Gilson was a revelation of his father's intellectual affections, and a short history of the Golden Age of Romanism, Bernard François Dominique.

Bernard Gilson had heard of Kierkegaard, but M. Jean Wall had not as yet lectured on the Danish Jeremiah in his classes. I related M. Jacques Maritain's answers to my queries concerning the present break between Protestantism and Romanism. The fault, Maritain had declared, had lain with the false concept of the Divine Right of Kings. I quoted Toynbee's view that an unbending papal absolutism had been the cause of the cleavage. Bernard Gilson regarded Toynbee's comment, and Dostoyevsky's criticism of Romanism as a continuation in religious form of the Roman Empire, as unjustified.

Bernard spoke to the theme of Protestant-Roman reunion with fine insight. There was important common ground between the two Communions, he acknowledged, particularly where Protestants continued to believe in the Deity of Christ. Creedal unanimity was thus reasonably established. Nonetheless, it was not possible, in his estimation, for reunion to materialize in view of wide divergence on the Sacraments. He considered this the most important disagreement. On this issue papal authority had been rejected by Protestants. Before reunion could occur, the Pope's right to decide disputed questions would have to be duly acknowledged. On the other hand, he could see no reason why the parliamentary principle might not be admitted into the administration of the Roman Church, provided only that the superior authority of the Pope were preserved.

Bernard Gilson did not feel competent to discuss the problems of Protestantism, but listened interestedly, and with apparent sympathy, to my outline of M. Maritain's suggestion — urging a renewal of spiritual and intellectual seriousness. Thinking politically, Bernard believed classical Christianity could approve any regime which sought to apply Christian charity in common sense solutions to social problems. He considered, he said, that even a dictatorship was not necessarily alien to Christian purposes, provided it respected the integrity of the individual. On this point, he acknowledged, there might be considerable debate. In any case he was convinced that social and economic democracy were of the very structure and spirit of classical Christianity.

At the dinner hour Bernard Gilson seemed loath to discontinue our interview. However, lest I miss his father at the Conseil de la Republique, I left at once. My taxi transported me through the rain to the French Senat, but the efficient effort of a secretary to locate M. Etienne Gilson in the halls or in the restaurant of the great building disclosed only that he had just departed.

Following dinner at my hotel I phoned to ascertain whether M. Gilson was free to receive me. In accordance with his gracious invitation I returned at nine o'clock. Etienne Gilson himself answered the bell, and ushered me at once into his study. It had been a long day; I had returned from Rome in the morning, after two nights and a day on the Simplon Orient Express; I had attended an afternoon lecture on Montaigne at the Sorbonne; I was weary in body and mind. After the stimulating evening with M. Gilson, however, who proved both a friendly conversationalist and a magnanimous host, I felt as refreshed as though a new day had begun.

M. Gilson agreed with Maritain that the Danish Pascal, Kierkegaard, had been truly a hero of faith, a mystic, but believed him also an important Christian philosopher; he had been the first in any significant degree to turn the Socratic dialectic to Christian account. There was greater similarity between Bernard and Kierkegaard, at the point of Christian inwardness, than between Thomas and the Dane.

Etienne Gilson was intrigued by Maritain's idea, as I reported it, that Thomas' philosophy had been basically existential. From

11

his own viewpoint, however, the problem of essence was inevitably prior to that of existence. He acknowledged, nonetheless, wide similarity of content between Maritain and himself. A new book of his own, in process of publication, he explained, specifically re-defined the problem of being.

I mentioned to M. Gilson that his volume, *The Spirit Of Mediaeval Philosophy,* had been introduced by Edwin Lewis to his classes at Drew University with admiration and affection. He was pleased at this tribute from a major American theologian, and amused when I informed him that Stanley Romaine Hopper, also of Drew, in his striking volume, *The Crisis Of Faith,* had suggested a strong tie between the Gilson philosophy and the neo-Plotinian mysticism of Bernard and the Victorines. He regarded it an honor, he said, to be called a neo-Plotinian.

We might at this point have discussed the desire, among mystics, to rise into the ecstasy of the Divine Embrace without passing through the crisis of repentance, and, as well, the tendency, after the manner of Hinduism, to look upon the Ojective of the Christian Pilgrimage as Union rather than as Fellowship with God. These elements in neo-Plotinianism Stanley R. Hopper has examined with critical penetration.

Seeking my host's opinion, I outlined Arnold J. Toynbee's discussion of fifteenth century papal intractability as the determining cause of the Reformation and its end product, Nationalism. M. Gilson spoke of the theme with magnanimity of mind. Toynbee's statement was unquestionably true, he said, yet it was necessary to consider exactly how the inclusion of the parliamentary principle would have affected the Roman Church. Had the parliamentary modification been accepted, Romanism would have assumed the fissiparous character of Protestantism. Beyond any doubt the Roman Church was an Absolute Despotism, asserted Gilson. It could not escape authoritarianism, if it were faithful to its Divine Commission. On a recent visit to the Vatican, M. Gilson had been impressed, he said, by the sheer Despotism of the Holy See. "Nobody had any authority except the Pope and his secretary." Yet if papal absolutism had been replaced by a Roman parliament, the Church undoubtedly would have undergone Protestantism's protean change. Authoritarian unity had given objective continuity to Roman Christianity, and saved it from anarchic disintegration. Nonetheless, M. Gilson acknowledged, the Reformation had swept away many abuses in the Roman Church, malpractices which had merited all the criticism they had received.

It was not to be understood that Christian thought possessed no living continuity of its own. On the contrary, the continuity of the Christian tradition had risen through an inevitable recognition of common convictions. Papal authority, however, had served admirably as a unifying force, a common court of appeal, without which the unity of tradition might, conceivably, have been shattered.

I called attention in some detail to Dostoyevsky's criticism, expressed in all his works, but perhaps most strongly in *The Idiot* and *The Brothers Karamazov,* that the Roman Church had accepted the political sword which Christ rejected in the Third Temptation. M. Gilson expressed his appreciation for Dostoyevsky. However, in his opinion, one had to decide whether or not Christ meant to influence the government of this world. If He did not intend to eliminate political evils in the here and now, Rome was wrong in her effort throughout history to make His influence felt realistically in the total life of succeeding generations. On the other hand, if Christ did mean that His will be executed on earth as in Heaven, Rome was right in her perpetual endeavor to enclose the State within the Church.

I reminded M. Gilson of the Protestant distinction between an influence exerted upon political life by Christian criticism and counsel, and the divergent influence brought to bear through political intrigue. He recognized this distinction, and freely acknowledged the moral hazard involved in the exercise of political power, but inclined to the view that, if policies were judged by their purposes, and if political power were recognized as properly subordinate to spiritual power, Rome's historic participation in European politics had been entirely defensible. Roman political involvement had been inescapably necessary, for without papal leadership the nations had proven themselves sheep without a shepherd.

13

What basic hindrances thwarted Protestant-Roman reunion? I asked. M. Gilson replied that Papacy, Sacraments, and Creed were issues of significance. However, in his estimation, the determining divergence appeared in distinct definitions of the Church. To Protestants, the Church was Christ in the individual — a subjective matter, while to Romans the Church itself was Christ — an objective affair. Protestants returned to the Bible and would have no intermediate authority. As a volume for devotional reading, the Bible served admirably without authoritative interpretation. But if a Protestant asked questions as he read, he could not but feel himself alone in his attempt to find convincing answers. A Roman recognized that he was not alone, that the Church, the contemporary Christ, had made and continued to make competent interpretations, informing him reliably concerning the true meaning of passages in question. In the Roman Communion the final authority in Biblical interpretation was the contemporary Church, centered in the Papacy. In Protestant Communions the final authority was the individual — hence Protestantism's intellectual variety, or, if you preferred, anarchy. The objective, and the subjective Church — this constituted the yawning gulf between Christendom's two halves; how indeed could another than a Parliamentary bridge be constructed across the chasm?

It would not be accurate, obviously, to describe Romanism as without subjective faith. Similarly, it would not be accurate to describe Protestantism as without an objective Church. Protestant Articles of Faith, constructed of classical Christianity, whether or not alive in the minds of pastors and people, are certainly objective, and Protestant administrative organizations objective as well. The World Council of Churches, at Amsterdam and New Delhi, now representing 192 denominations, and 300,000,000 members of Christian Churches, with 50,000,000 in Russian dominated countries, has united a vast Parliament with free personal Commitment. Yet it is true that the unmistakable foundation of Romanism is papal and authoritarian, of Protestantism personal and libertarian.

Speaking to the theme of Protestant renewal, M. Gilson felt that the main problem was a decision one way or the other about Christianity. Was Protestantism determined to serve Christianity,

14

or some other religion of its own invention? If it decided against Christianity, it could then comfortably forbear Evangelism; if for Christianity, its Evangelism would have to be of renewed intensity. Christianity could not escape being Evangelistic; when it had ceased to be Evangelistic, it had ceased to be Christian. A straightforward return to Christian theology, and an equally unashamed return to great zeal in pressing the Christian invitation to pagan societies and pagan souls — these were obvious Protestant needs. A recovery of Evangelism could not come to pass until there first occurred a recovery of the Christian Faith.

Politically speaking, there was nothing in Christianity to prevent Christians from voting as Socialists. In M. Gilson's estimation, Christianity was politically neutral; it sought only a Christian use of existing political machinery. Christianity could have no common ground with Marxian materialism, nor with Marxian class antagonism, nor with Marxian totalitarianism, yet the clear meaning of Christian charity was social responsibility. Only irresponsibility would allow common economic injustices to continue unchecked. Nations in straitened postwar circumstances could not afford lawless raids upon their slender stores. Social controls, even with the hazards involved, were obvious necessities. Moderate Socialism, with personal freedom, was simply an intelligent facing of reality.

I mentioned that I planned to interview Christopher Dawson and C. S. Lewis. Etienne Gilson expressed profound admiration for both writers, showing me their books on his shelves. He regarded Lewis a pure theologian. He asked me to convey his affectionate greeting to Dawson, whom he considered one of mankind's greater historians.

CHRISTOPHER DAWSON

Perhaps it is the influence of geography on ideas, but England has long proven that it is at a distance from Rome. Even Romanism in England is English, notably modified from the French, and even more from the Italian. Christopher Dawson's inclusiveness of perspective, his critical honesty, are impressive. He writes and speaks like a particularly literate and particularly liberal Protestant.

There is no slavishness toward papal authority, no nicely preserved lip service, rather a deep affection, formed in freedom, for the living symbol of Roman Union. He thinks of Christ as Lord and Pope as Servant. As he suggested, there are at least two Catholicisms, one centered in the Vatican, the other centered in Christ.

Christina Dawson, his daughter, received me at the lovely home on Boars Hill, west of Oxford, and provided me at my request with her father's book, *The Judgment of The Nations*. She placed me in a deck chair on the south terrace, overlooking the lawn and the roses, to await the return of her father and mother from an interview with Mr. Sheed, the New York publisher. Christina was engaged in packing, for the family was off on the morrow to holiday in Devonshire. I offered to "sit on the lid" with my two hundred and four pounds, but Christina explained, smiling with great charm, that many items were yet to be assembled before the cases could be closed. I described my visit in Paris with Etienne Gilson and his son, Bernard. With fine thoughtfulness, she grasped at once the solution to Bernard's problem of a place in Oxford for future study, giving me the name and address of a French student center at the University.

Mrs. Dawson graciously invited me to tea. The restfulness of the hour of family fellowship was most welcome, for I had reached Oxford from London at four in the morning and had risen at eight to begin the full day.

When Christopher Dawson led me to his private study, a meeting of minds had already taken place; it was possible forthwith to begin the serious interview. I therefore asked: "Can a parliamentary bridge be constructed across the chasm separating Roman objectivism from Protestant subjectivism?" In Mr. Dawson's *The Judgment Of The Nations* I had noted considerable emphasis on the prior necessity of unified spiritual leadership if political and economic peace were to become realities. Christianity's Universal Church had created Western Civilization (Dawson and Toynbee were of one mind); only a Universal Church could save Europe from Nationalism. He had urged unity not only among Protestants but also between Protestantism and

16

Romanism, secondarily in organization, primarily in common consciousness of the Kingship of Christ. Perhaps the fissiparous trend in Christendom had run its course.

Mr. Dawson at once declared that Roman Christianity could not be described as purely objective. Had there not been any number of mystics in the Roman Communion, men of the stature of Thomas A. Kempis? I was reminded that both Susanah and John Wesley had read *The Imitation Of Christ* from childhood, that the same classic had been my own spiritual mainstay. Surely Christian inwardness was not exclusively Protestant. Mr. Dawson asserted that Protestantism was not merely subjective; the Ecumenical movement clearly evidenced a strong desire for objective unity.

Kierkegaardian subjectivism had not been typically Protestant, in Dawson's opinion. It had been against the objectivism of the Danish Established Church that Kierkegaard had revolted, as Wesley had revolted, in an earlier day, against the Anglican Establishment.

In support of my characterization of the Roman Church as basically objective, I quoted Gilson's statement to me: "The Church to a Protestant is Christ in the individual; to a Roman the Church itself is Christ." I quoted also Gilson's remark that the papacy was a sheer despotism, and the assertion of Pius XII, reported by Maritain in Rome, that civil authority came from the people, but papal authority from God. Briefly I narrated the amusing reply of a Roman cameo salesman to my question about Italian Communism: "There is very little Communism in Italy. We Italians are all Christians; we believe in the Pope — and religion, in that order." Mr. Dawson smiled at the anecdote, but regarded the papacy a necessary symbol of a unified Christendom, as England's Kings or Queens were wholesome symbols of a unified Empire. This characterization served to underscore the divergence between the nominal authority of a British monarch and the absolutism of the Vatican, and afforded me the opportunity to cite Toynbee's argument that the fifteenth century papal rejection of parliamentary authority had provoked the so-called Reformation. Mr. Dawson was convinced that Toynbee, with whom as historian and philosopher he has so much in common, had over-simplified the pre-Reformation problem. In Dawson's opinion, irrationalism and revolution had been seething everywhere among the people; these explosive forces had shattered Christian unity.

And what, I asked, of Dostoyevsky's attack on Romanism as the acceptance of the political sword rejected by Christ? Mr. Dawson suggested that *The Grand Inquisitor* in *The Brothers Karamazov* could be interpreted as an attack not upon Romanism but rather upon Nihilism. In his view, Dostoyevsky had been reaching out for a genuine Christian philosophy. I reminded him that in *The Idiot* the attack upon Rome had been specific, and by name: Romanism's political intrigues, according to the Russian thinker, had made atheists or protestants of all honest men. Yes, said Dawson correctly, but *The Karamazovs* had been a later work. Still, said I, even in *The Karamazovs* you had Ivan's vigorous statement: "The Church must not become the State (that is, priests must not rule), but the State must become the Church (responsive to the Church's moral leadership)." I mentioned that this idea seemed not far removed from T. S. Eliot's *The Idea of a Christian Society*, nor from Dawson's own statement, in *The Judgment Of The Nations:* "The God-State has been the greatest Enemy of God."

The Roman Church, said Christopher Dawson, had not wielded the political sword; even in the Inquisition persons condemned by the Church had been handed over to civil authorities for punishment. And one should never lose sight of the two Romanisms, the uncritical and the critical. Throughout the history of the Church there had always been critics, like Dante, articulate in opposition to papal military ventures. Dante had not hesitated in *The Divine Comedy* to consign immoral popes to the Inferno, yet he had never questioned papal authority in matters of Faith.

Maritain, I reported, had asserted that the Protestant Reformation had been evoked by the false idea of the Divine Right of Kings. In Dawson's estimation, there had been something wholesome in the notion of the Divine right of kings — at least the recognition that all authority had come from God. Mr. Dawson had been impressed, he said, by the British Coronation Service, preserved from the centuries. George VI and Elizabeth II had thus received their authority from God by consecration to His will, had indeed actually received the Crown from the Church, had accepted their responsibility as Defenders of the Faith.

There seemed little possibility of harmony between Protestant insistence upon parliamentary power, and Roman insistence upon papal absolutism. Complete agreement existed only in the common conception of the Church as Mediator of the moral Love of God, of ethical seriousness, to societies and souls.

What of the Protestant idea, I enquired, that Christ's Church was one Great Tree of Faith, with many legitimate Branches? Mr. Dawson was pleased that this unifying idea existed among Protestants. Christ, he said, was clearly the Trunk or Root of the Tree of Life. However, the Roman communion's idea seemed defensible that throughout its numerous national Churches and its various Orders, Franciscan, Dominican, Jesuit, and the like, it constituted the Entire Tree. To Roman folk, Protestantism seemed a Growth of a different kind.

If Mr. Dawson's expressed idea be accepted, that Christ, as God and Man, is the Basis of Union in Christendom, are not Protestant Churches, committed nominally and actually to one or another interpretation of this Faith, necessarily Branches of the legitimate Tree? The argument could be carried further. For example, if the Kingship of Christ is accepted as the Basis of union, what hinders the membership of the Roman Church in the parliamentary World Council of Churches? The Ecumenical organization uniformly receives into its fellowship any denomination willing to confess its "faith in Christ as God and Saviour"? Indeed, this would seem the simpler path to Christian reunion. A Pope of adventurous disposition might in truth make exactly this brave crossing of the Rubicon, thereby proving himself, in one magnanimous deed, "the Servant of the Servants of Christ."

What counsel, I enquired, would Christopher Dawson give to Protestants seeking the renewal of central Christianity in their midst? My own Methodism, I reported, had been described with superficial justification as a mere crusade for Prohibition and Pacifism — neither a bad idea. As a parochial student had put it,

19

not incorrectly: "Due to Methodism, peace was raging throughout the country." American Congregationalism too, it appeared, had not won a decisive victory against autonomous Capitalism. What precisely was to be done to re-invigorate Christianity in Protestantism? Mr. Dawson expressed his regret if the deistic substitution of respectability for Christianity had captured American denominations. No simple remedy had been found for theological malnutrition. Perhaps, I suggested, disintegration on the one hand could be countered by integration on the other — what Sorokin calls the "integral" point of view. Serious Christianity would assuredly prove a positive force in a universe of negation. Mr. Dawson believed that new techniques were needed for the Christian re-invigoration of Christendom — of meditation and prayer for individual spiritual renewal, of mass education for intellectual recovery. The Study Retreat had proven effective in both endeavors. Christians thus withdrew from the world for intellectual and spiritual cultivation; they received new vitality of mind and spirit without which religious awakenings had no permanence. This sounded like Maritain's emphasis upon intellectual *and* spiritual renewal, or like Brunner's insistence upon "a live theology." The Study Retreat, I reported, was already widely in use in American Protestantism, particularly among young people, though it could not always have been affirmed that "faith in Christ as God and Saviour," in those terms, had been paramount, or even articulate, at these assemblies. Frequently, to my knowledge, leardership had seemed divided among Autonomists in philosophy, Deists in religion, and Utopianists in politics.

Deism was dominant neither in England nor on the Continent, Mr. Dawson asserted. Few leaders, as far as he knew, had bogged down in the morass of half-belief. Europeans were either Theists and Incarnationists or more concerned with Enquiry than Ontology. No intermediate position had gained respect.

Politically, said Dawson, a classical Christian might go as far left as spiritual freedom would permit. Political machinery, whether of the left or of the right, could be used with moral responsibility and Christian charity for or against the human spirit. Social planning, an intelligent approach to group problems, was not in itself alien to Christian purposes.

Spiritual freedom is indeed the yardstick by which many political, and religious, institutions have been measured and found wanting. I stopped awhile at the foot of Oxford's exquisite monument to the memory of Cranmer, Ridley, and Latimer, martyrs for spiritual freedom in Bloody Mary's day. The inscription on the shaft seems of permanent significance:

> To the Glory of God and in Grateful Commemoration of His Servants, Thomas Cranmer, Nicholas Ridley, and Hugh Latimer, Prelates of the Church of England, Who near this spot yielded their bodies to be burned, bearing witness to the sacred Truths which they had affirmed and maintained against the errors of the Church of Rome, and rejoicing that to them it was given not only to believe in Christ, but also to suffer for His sake, this monument was erected by public subscription in the year of Our Lord MDCCCXLI.

I remembered the man of Oxford whom Queen Elizabeth called "our father Foxe," a lifelong fugitive from bigotry. His classic account, of martyrs tortured by the Roman Empire and the Roman Church, remains documentary evidence that spiritual freedom has not been cheaply achieved.

In any case, it would be hard to find a simpler basis for united spiritual leadership in the modern world than Christopher Dawson's definition of a Christian as a man with faith in Christ, and of the true Church as obedient to Christ as King. If, on these definitions, Protestantism and Romanism cannot meet in brotherly embrace, as Allies in a common cause, there is need for honest searching of the soul; it could only be because one or the other, or both, in point of fact, have substituted some lesser King for Christ. If Roman Christians have made an Idol of the Papal Church, have Protestant Christians made an Idol of the Nationalist State, or, for better or worse, of Individual Opinion? Holy Community would seem a better alternative than Sheer Communism, Sheer Romanism, or Sheer Chaos.

21

G. K. CHESTERTON and DOROTHY COLLINS

I had heard of G. K. Chesterton, it seemed, all my life, and every idea attributed to him had always informed and amused me at one and the same time, but the first book of his to come into my hands had been *Orthodoxy*. I had found it quite the most hilarious book on serious Christianity I had ever seen, and the hilarity, surprisingly enough, had not been an alien element forcibly incorporated but had risen out of the seriousness itself. I know of no book like it to this day. The paradoxical quality of Chesterton's quick mind, and of his profound thought, had fascinated me. No one ought to be allowed to remain a Churchmember for long without being invited to read him. His basic ideas, and some of his expressions, have continued to impress me. Chesterton, it developed, had not been converted to Christianity by evangelists but by atheists and freethinkers, who had succeeded in arousing in him doubts deeper than their own, namely, doubts of Doubt as a sufficient substitute for Faith. It had dawned upon Chesterton that Christianity, damned from the one side for its supine meekness, and damned with equal vehemence from the other for its crusading and bloodthirsty imperialism, was obviously in the middle of the road. He had discovered that Christianity did not seek to merge all the elements of life into a distinctionless amalgam; rather it raised each element to its own highest pitch and held it from distortion by balancing it with others similarly heightened. It intensified passion, but balanced it with a strengthened control and a spiritual love. It increased man's respect for himself, yet deepened his loathing of his egoism. "Insofar as I am man, I am the chief of creatures; insofar as I am *a* man, I am the chief of sinners." Orthodoxy, in Chesterton's picture, had not been a strait-laced spinster; rather she had been the jovial and kindly and competent mother of a large and lusty family. Orthodoxy, I had learned, was not partiality, for partiality was heresy. Heresy was not belief in something untrue, but belief in something true — a truth, however, wrenched loose from the total cluster of truths and exalted to a monistic absolute, a lonely eminence not properly its own. Paul Elmer More similarly described heresy in *The Demon Of The*

Absolute. Orthodoxy was precisely the total cluster of truths in living relationship. "The Church had to be careful, if only that the world might be careless." To have succumbed to any one of the numerous historic heresies, whether Gnosticism with its excessive otherworldliness or Arianism with its excessive thisworldliness, would have been easy. The amazing thing about the Christian Church, as G. K. had put it, was that She had executed the difficult balancing act called Orthodoxy, as She had traveled at break-neck speed through the world, "the dull heresies sprawling on all sides, the wild truth reeling but erect." "It is easy to let the age have its head; the difficult thing is to keep one's own."

The Christ, as G. K. had known Him, with the deep understanding of faith and love, had not been the collected absence, but the collected presence, of vital human emotions. He had been as tender as a child, as meek as a lamb, but, upon occasion, had "flung furniture down the front steps of the Temple." G. K.'s Christ had not been the emaciated "female consumptive" pictured by many painters, but full-blooded and alive, hiding but one thing from His disciples — what G. K. believed to have been "a smile."

Innumerable college students had read G. K.'s volumes at my assignment, and written for the most part wholly admirable essays upon his basic ideas. Invariably the class-room reading of an essay about G. K. had been a red-letter event of rich humor and deep insight, a feast of mind and soul.

With all this in mind, it was unthinkable that I should be in England and not make my pilgrimage to Top Meadow at Beaconsfield, where the great human, the laughing saint, had lived joyously and humbly with Mrs. Chesterton from 1922 till his death in 1936. Dorothy Collins, the secretary, who had waited upon both Mr. and Mrs. G. K. hand and foot for so many years, had joined them there. I had no idea who, or what, I would find, for Mrs. Chesterton had died two years after her husband, and there had been no children.

My journey, however, could not have been better timed, and I must pay a tribute to the remarkable efficiency of my guiding Angel, for I arrived, entirely without advance information, as an annual lecture was being delivered in the single great hall which

23

had once served as G. K.'s living room, dining room, and bedroom. The lecturer was Dom Ignatius Rice, headmaster of a nearby Catholic Boys' School, the very priest who had received G. K. into the Roman Church. The room was well filled with G. K.'s admirers from far and near. The event was sponsored by the Catholic Aid Society, now operating the Chesterton Home as a refuge and rehabilitation center for converted Protestant clergymen.

G. K.'s courage and humility were emphasized in the lecture. Three humorous stories were narrated, in addition to the familiar one about the telegram to Mrs. Chesterton: "Am in Paddington Station: where ought I to be?" One anecdote concerned a conversation preceding a Chesterton lecture. The chairman, full of advance alibis for the childish queries which might follow the discourse, had said: "I'm afraid the questions which will be asked will be silly, Mr. Chesterton." G. K. had immediately replied: "Not half as silly as my answers. . . ." On another occasion Dom Rice had accompanied G. K. to a lecture platform. When the humorist had risen to speak, he had taken a very small notebook from his vest pocket, opened it with great ostentation, placed it with care on the table before him, and never looked at it again throughout his talk. Furthermore, nothing had been written in the notebook . . . G. K. had once been engaged in a debate with a learned antagonist. After his own first speech, as the scholar had endeavored to present his weighty arguments, G. K. had removed a long carving knife from his coat and, with the attention of the audience fully turned toward him, had leisurely sharpened the point on the tiniest stub of a pencil.

A London friend, Anne Marie Gresham,[1] with the wit and charm of Ireland, explained to me the work of the Catholic Aid Society, and thoughtfully presented me to Dorothy Collins.

Seated by Miss Collins in Top Meadow's sixty-foot living room, with G. K.'s books and pictures about, I sought from her his possible answers to many questions. An attempt to define G. K.'s Catholicism in terms of Thomas Aquinas, Augustine, Erigena, or

1. Read her brief autobiography in our book, *These Found The Way* (Westminster Press).

24

Pascal seemed to lead precisely nowhere, and perhaps for the obvious reason that G. K.'s Christianity could not otherwise be defined than as Chestertonian. His swing to Romanism had been due simply to what he regarded as the sterility and frustration of an essentially solipsistic Protestantism with its shattering influence upon theological and political community.

What hope, then, if any, would he have seen for a renewal of central Christianity within Protestantism, should a common will exist to produce it? Miss Collins, herself a Roman convert from Anglicanism, was quite sure that G. K. would have seen no hope at all for Protestantism. She cited his reply to the letter of an admirer, who had indicated that Chesterton had converted him to Christianity. G. K. had urged the man to follow him "the whole way" into the Roman Church. I could not but remember G. K.'s characterization of Protestant denominations as "booby-traps," misleading the simple and beguiling the wise either into heresy or anarchy. Protestantism's only hope, Miss Collins was certain, lay in a return to the Roman Fold.

But, I insisted, would not G. K. have had a word of counsel for those who shared his Faith but could not in good conscience share his Church? The anarchic and solipsistic hazards of Protestantism were obvious, I pointed out; yet if in all honesty a genuine Christian believer could not support Roman authoritarianism, would not G. K. have had a message for him? To the Protestant Christian, the hazards of papal despotism were greater than the hazards of democracy.

Miss Collins considered this question a moment, then replied that Protestantism, in her estimation, could have no future unless it could agree about its central beliefs. Through some parliamentary procedure, perhaps like that of the early Councils of Nicea and Chalcydon, Protestantism needed to establish an outline of common convictions. Clearly Protestantism could not survive with neither beliefs nor convictions. Who could preach the absence of an idea? If a Protestant Supreme Court or Ecumenical Council on Theology and Life could be assembled, Protestantism might rediscover its characteristic Ideas, and thus provide the people with an affirmative message. Otherwise, what hope could there be? On any other basis, the fissiparous process in Protestant theology and in Protestant organization would continue into infinity, if not into absurdity.

I related briefly the story of the World Council of Churches, a fellowship of 112 (now 192) non-Roman denominations, possibly representing a majority of the world's Christians, providing exactly the needed rallying center for Protestantism through its articulate faith in Christ as, in a profound and unique sense, "God and Saviour," accenting the underlining unity in the Holy Spirit of all believers. There could be, after all, but one Church of Christ, and if the Roman Church were shepherding its great part of the One Flock in an authoritarian fashion, non-Roman Catholicism was sheperding its equal or greater part of the same Flock in a parliamentary manner. Miss Collins was not familiar with the World Council, but, as I presented it, believed it a step in the right direction, implying that the second right step would be submission to Rome. She declared that Protestants misunderstood the idea of papal infallibility, a principle which applied to papal decisions upon disputed doctrines, only when such disputes were brought to him for settlement. The last such decision had been given in 1870; appeals were not common occurrences. Any good ship needed a captain, authorized to render final decisions in emergencies. How could a Great Ocean Liner follow more than one Course? . . . If Roman Catholicism can properly be likened to a sea-going vessel, I suggested, might not Protestantism be compared to a City built upon land, governed not by Captain but by Council?

Would Miss Collins say a word, I asked, concerning G. K.'s political philosophy? She mentioned his term, "Distributism." He had opposed centralization and bureaucracy, had felt that political and economic controls were moving farther and farther from the people. Power, both economic and political, should return to the people, who were, after all, most deeply concerned. The small people should own their own land and their own souls. Government could serve Distributism chiefly by curtailing its own omnipotence, and by guaranteeing to each man his equal share of the soil. Socialism continually moved ownership and control from human beings to hierarchies.

Miss Collins' deepest memory of G. K. was of his child-like humility, his complete selflessness of spirit. I left Top Meadow reluctantly, with renewed love for the great Controversialist, and in prayer. He understood the meaning of Christian love, as few men have understood it, when he said: "At every moment we are wholly dependent upon God. When a man realizes that he can never pay the debt he owes to God, he will be forever trying. He will always be throwing things away into a pit of unfathomable thanks."

THE WORLD COUNCIL POINT OF VIEW

MARC BOEGNER

But for my friend, Andre Poulain, pastor of the Reformed Church in Dieppe, I would have missed the vigorous and colorful administrator, Marc Boegner, whose titles are virtually without end, and whose original ideas are as spiritual as they are practical. The American ecclesiastical administrator has not uniformly impressed either clergy or laity with his intellectual depth. He sometimes has been said, no doubt unjustly, to resemble the successful politician. It was doubly refreshing therefore to meet an individual who, in true continental fashion, had achieved specialized competence in organizational mechanics, but at the same time epitomized spiritual leadership at its best. He was wide awake to social problems, equally wide awake to controversies involving the central ideas of the Christian Faith, and deeply concerned that an adequate bridge might speedily be constructed from the Churches and their healing Christ to the masses of France and the world. He was clearly anxious, not so much to introduce the masses to the Church as to introduce the mind of Christ to the masses, and this anxiety endeavored to assist me.

Marc Boegner, then President of the Reformed Church in France, President of the French Council of Churches, and one President, as well, of the World Council of Churches, was not in his office at 47, rue de Clichy, when I called at 2:30 P.M. A friendly individual informed me that Pasteur Boegner would return to his office at 4:00 o'clock. The hour and a half of waiting gave at first every prospect of tedium, but, as often happens, proved in the event to be filled with light. I made my way up four flights to the office of Jean Paul Benoit, head of the Society for Evangelism

28

of the French Reformed Church. The entrance disclosed a room filled with books and pamphlets whose titles uniformly indicated that Evangelism, as understood by the French Reformed Church, had something to do with personal commitment to Christ as Saviour and Lord. Several good people appeared, but could make little of my French. After a time an elderly gentleman, under the impression that he spoke English, did his best with patient charity to understand me and answer my questions. He had been in the office for Evangelism more than twenty years, he said, and, since M. Benoit was then in the north of France preaching, he would endeavour to assist me.

In particular I learned from Pasteur Jacques Krug that the ideological center of Evangelism, as understood by the Reformed Church of France, was stated most simply in John 3:16: "For God so loved the world that He gave His only begotten Son." M. Krug directed my attention to these words, in French, in the opening paragraph of the Society's declaration of purpose. I learned also that the Society, under M. Krug's direction, published an annual book of devotions, containing one page for each day in the year, and entitled: "Une Parole Pour Tous" (A Word For All). The French "Parole" fascinated me. At my request M. Krug turned the pages of his French Bible to John 1:1, and there, in bold type, was "Parole" for "Logos". "In the beginning was the Parole." Any philologist could thus develope a thinklette sermon on the theme: "In the beginning — Grace." The daily devotional booklet clearly offered a diet of meat and wine and honey rather than of thin gruel. I learned further from Jacques Krug that there were two types of Churches organized by the Society for Evangelism: Churches of Conservation, designed to consolidate new area gains on a self-supporting basis, and Churches of Conquest, small cells established in private homes supported by the Society and staffed by specially trained pastors. Through its Churches of Conquest the Society, in one hundred and thirty years of existence, had added many permanent Congregations to French Protestantism. In addition, a pastor in the south of France had devoted several summers to street-preaching and home-visitation in nearby villages.

Elsewhere a smart auto-trailer circulated through French towns with Christian literature. The Society's effort to educate the French masses was clearly no empty gesture.

Pasteur Jacques Delpech, Secretary General of the Society, appeared at this point, and with his excellent English, and gracious spirit, greatly extended my knowledge, and deepened my appreciation, of French Protestantism.

The problem of nominal versus actual Christianity was by no means absent from the French Reformed Church, M. Delpech asserted, yet the many rather than the few were seriously committed to the Christian ordering of their lives in obedience to the Spirit of Christ. There were no Fundamentalists among the pastors, though a few who attempted "to out-Barth Barth." Predominantly the pastors were Barthians or Neo-Calvinists, convinced that evil was mixed with good in human hearts, that social and personal salvation could come only from the God of Power and Grace Who gave Himself to mankind in Judea and Galilee. The God Who spoke from the Cross and the Empty Tomb, in the Sermon on the Mount and on the Mount of Transfiguration, he said, could bring good out of man's unrighteousness. Man's task was to hear and obey the Divine Word, recognizing his insufficiency without the aid of the Holy Spirit. Only thus might man impart the Divine Life to society.

To enable me to understand the present state of the French Reformed Church, M. Delpech outlined its history. In 1809 Bonaparte gave the Huguenots a Concordat, relieving them from persecution and listing their pastors among State employees. In all probability this gratuity of Bonaparte had been given less from a desire to propagate Christianity than from a shrewd plan to diminish the political power of the Roman Church. In any case the Church of the Huguenots became thus an Established French denomination. In the mid-nineteenth century a great revival broke out, considerably enlarging the Church's membership. Some Congregations, blessed with the new vitality, became Free Churches, refusing longer to accept State funds for the support of the Gospel. In 1905, with the revocation of the Concordat, French Protestantism found itself under the fortunate necessity of living on its own vitality. The various Congregations, Methodist, Presbyterian, and the like, remained separate until 1938, when, in the atmosphere of fellowship provided by the growing World Council of Churches, they united with the Huguenots in the Reformed Church of France. Today, but for a handful of nonconformist Congregations, there are but two Protestant denominations, the Lutherans and the Reformed, numbering between them a million members.

This would seem a practical program of possible union for Evangelical denominations in America—following E. Stanley Jones' idea of Federal Union, like the United States, or another similar in point and purpose. Only the worship of the husks of tradition, an unworthy veneration which Toynbee calls Archaism—an attempt to turn time backward in its flight—keeps apart the American Protestant denominations committed, like the World Council of Churches, to "faith in Christ as, on one or another interpretation, God and Savior." Classical Christianity in its Parliamentarian or Protestant form is One, by interior commitment to the Kingship of Christ and by external departure from Romanism. If Evangelical Protestantism is in fact united, by common separation from secularism on the one hand, and from Romanism on the other, what is there to keep its constituent denominations apart? Divergent denominations, born of unholy wedlock between classical Christianity and various sovereign States, may once have served useful national purposes, but within America have what further reason, other than direct personal and congregational vitality, for separation? How can the world be united politically when the Community of Christ is divided? Has the United Nations, from Woodrow Wilson's early effort to its present growing reality, proceeded farther toward Free World Community than the Churches of Christ?

Politically speaking, M. Delpech continued, France was divided among Romanists, Socialists, and Communists. Members of the Reformed Church were mainly to be found in the various Socialist-Democratic parties. Now and then a Communist became a Christian, and if he did so seriously, since there was no compulsion for him to do so otherwise, within a few months or years

31

his interest normally shifted from a secular to a modestly-religious program, from Collectivism to Community. Few members of the Reformed Church were supporters of the Romanist Party.

A strange fact in modern times was the recent emergence of many vigorous Evangelicals among Roman priests. They constituted a minority, to be sure, but were a wholesome sign of common spiritual resurrection. These Roman Evangelicals would be perfectly at home, and warmly welcomed, he said, in any Protestant pulpit.

In my opinion, the future belongs to the Free World Mind, released alike from secular sterility and idolatrous despotism.

Shortly after 4:00 P.M. I returned to the Foyer of Pasteur Boegner's office. While waiting, I copied on a scrap of paper the following striking sentence, printed in large letters over a doorway, credited to one Pasteur Tommy Fallou, leader in French Protestant social action:

La religion de Jesus Christ est tout a la fois spirituelle et sociale, spirituelle dans sa racine, sociale dans sa manifestation; l'activite sociale n'est donc pas un resultat plus ou moin accidentel de la pieta, elle eu est la consequence directe et necessaire.

The religion of Jesus Christ is always both spiritual and social, spiritual in its character, social in its manifestation; social activity is never a more or less accidental result of piety, it is rather a direct and necessary consequence.

An admirable summary of a classical Christian idea. As I read it, another gentleman appeared, whom also Andre Poulain had asked me to see, Pasteur Paul Conord, General Secretary of the Reformed Church of France. This splendid person invited me into his office, and tried with me, as desperately with his broken English as I with my broken French, to play host and guest. I learned that RELIGION IN LIFE, an American Journal,[1] came regularly through Pasteur Conord's office to interested French pastors, and, as well, THEOLOGY TODAY[2] from Princeton. At M. Conord's request, I sought to summarize three dominant Kier-

1. Which has carried my essays on Paul Elmer More, Soren A. Kierkegaard, Dorothy L. Sayers, and Arnold J. Toynbee.
2. Which has carried my essays on Dostoyevsky and Sorokin.

kegaardian ideas, but found no way to translate into idiomatic French, even with the aid of Pascal's "Wager", the idea of "the Leap".

As I struggled with translation difficulties, Pasteur Marc Boegner appeared and conducted me into his office. He was kind enough to solve the translation problem, borrowing a word from the race track to convey the thought to M. Conord. On Marc Boegner's desk lay a copy of the Protestant Journal, FOI ET VIE (WORD AND LIFE); its page of contents disclosed seven articles on the deity of Christ by French Protestants and one on the same theme by a Roman priest.

My first question to Pasteur Boegner concerned the principle of Ecumenicity. Did the World Council of Churches seek to bring together what God had put asunder? Not at all, asserted the President of the World Council. There was no desire to eliminate existing Protestant Communions. Each member denomination maintained its own theology and its independence of action. Nor was the World Council a super-Denomination, as the United Nations seemed, in his view, a super-State. Enemies of the World Council had declared it an attempt to swallow existing Evangelical Communions in a super-Sect, but the accusation had missed the point. The World Council was designed to do one thing only — to bring representatives of all Evangelical denominations to one council table, and Rome itself if possible, to discuss common problems and purposes. In an atmosphere of friendship, conscious alliance had been formed against common enemies and in support of common objectives. Recognition of the common Faith had already given Evangelical Protestantism increased effectiveness as an instrument of Divine Grace in the regeneration of humanity. A genuine working cooperation had been established; in time objective union might be achieved. Reunion was not in all cases desirable, in view of the comparatively greater flexibility and efficiency of small organizations. In many cases, however, member denominations had become aware, through the ministry of the Council, of the sin of disunion in the Body of Christ.

All this was very fine, I observed, but around what central Faith were member denominations united? It was a splendid thing for representatives of Buddhism, Judaism, and Christianity to come together in one room, in what Sorokin calls "spatial adjacency". It was another to achieve a significant ideological community across difference. Would not a pan-religious harmony prove short-lived if the Christian mentioned his characteristic beliefs? The Mind of the Universe, from Whom all moral religions had taken their being, in Whom all lived and moved, had often in fact and once fully become truly Man, the Christian believed; Christ the Lord had died on a Cross under the burden of Buddhists' as well as Christians' sub-humanity, had imparted to as many as received Him Power to become the sons of God.

The Old Testament disclosed the division of mankind at the Tower of Babylon, and that division, which men considered only a curse, may have been also a blessing; unity, constructed in the absence of common self-transcendence, forever rebuilds the Tower of Babel. To unite all religions in one nominal fellowship would not be as significant an achievement as to keep them creatively united, and permanent unity would necessarily involve a growing common ideology. The ideology would have to include a center in Christ or it would require one sacrifice which the Christian could not make, the sacrifice of the Kingship of Christ. Once the Christian had sacrificed Christ, in fact whether or not in name, would he be any longer a Christian? The Roman Emperors, with a measure of wisdom, in one sense only not unlike that of the United Nations, offered absolute equality to all religions. All accepted, honored by the Emperors' notice, except Christianity, which was not at liberty to deny Christ. As Arnold J. Toynbee has written with power, it was in part this basic exclusiveness, this provinciality, of Christianity which gave it the victory over its more amiable competitors, exactly as its parent, Judaism, had won the victory over its Syriac rivals in a similar race. The Unity of the Godhead, said Toynbee, could not otherwise be disclosed to man than through an exclusive, even a provincial, Revelation.

Because Christians believe that Christ was, and is, the Infinite in the Finite, God incarnate in Man, I suggested they could not, with integrity, surrender Him to gain the world. Even on the lesser ground of expediency, Christianity was not at liberty to deny its defining Center, though it must recognize One Father of all men, one transcendent and immanent Reality, in respectful community with secondary Centers, for, again in Toynbee's description, it was Christianity which found Western man a barbarian, a raw savage, and, by its gift of life, promoted him to his present Free World leadership. Was Western Society, even for the sake of unity, willing to surrender its Father, its Mother, its Power — its freedom of world and of soul?

Marc Boegner responded with vigor to this challenge. A few Americans, he said, and a negligible number of Europeans, had launched a pan-religious movement. Their purpose had been to reduce the glory of each religion to a watery fluid, and pour what was left into a common "soup". But real soup was nourishing, whereas this neutral gruel would have neither flavor, calories, nor vitamins. The World Council had a little, but only a little, fortunately or unfortunately, in common with any World Alliance for Secular Friendship, or a World Community of Mammon-worshippers. The latter, the surrender of Mind to Matter, of Freedom to Slavery, had enjoyed, in the Free World, no authentic life. The World Council of Churches had sought, in practice and charter, he said, "to bring together for common study and fellowship only denominations sincerely committed to faith in Christ as God and Saviour." This was the rallying ideology of the World Council, as it was of classical Christianity. Aside from this commitment, said Boegner, Evangelical Protestantism had no reason for existence. Upon this Rock Christ had built, was now building, and would continue to build His imperishable Church, one Congregation across all centuries, continents, and Communions, a Community of Mankind able to pray, at Christ's invitation, with different footnotes, "Our Father who art in Heaven," to recognize, in different ways and languages, through many Multi-verses, a single infinite Universe.

One tremendous challenge confronted contemporary Christianity, Boegner emphasized, the necessity of reaching the masses. The problem was specially acute in France, he asserted; contrary to usual belief the average Frenchman was a pagan simply. One million Protestants and eight million Romans were a minority. In this connection, I remembered that there appeared to be no French Sabbath. Throughout France all sorts of mercantile houses, even barber shops and dime stores, were open on Sunday with business going forward at mid-week pace. M. Boegner was convinced that in England and America, in some degree, religious education in childhood had given even the man in the street some recognition of Biblical names, some acquaintance with a Christian vocabulary; French children, in point of fact, he said, had been raised without religious instruction. The most ardent Evangel of Christ, speaking to the French masses, discovered that he was speaking in a foreign tongue. The people simply did not understand him. The original purpose of the pentecostal gift of tongues seemed reversed; the gift once given for the spread of the Gospel now prevented its spread. The masses saw but did not perceive, heard but did not understand. A major question concerned all Christian leaders: "How could a bridge most speedily be constructed from Christianity to the masses?"

I pointed out that religious illiteracy was not, as Pasteur Boegner had suggested, purely French. He had described with a measure of accuracy the American problem. Perhaps in England, the Cradle of Atlantic Democracy, religious delinquency was less prevalent.

In any case, Schweitzer or other methods had to be found for building the bridge — whether in England, America, France, Germany, Russia, or Africa. Many immediate steps, said Pasteur Boegner, were under consideration. He planned in the near future to attend a conference of French leaders particularly concerned to find a way to the people.

We did not discuss the point, but on reflection it seems that the need is not merely an external matter of devices and techniques, rather a growing universal commitment to the Free World Mind of Christ. The Spirit of Truth alone can mobilize human strength sufficiently to achieve the Great End. For this Leardership men, in all tongues, pray with earnestness. Paul and Barnabas thus built their historic bridge to the troubled Hellenic Civilization. Many historic periods of Christian resurrection were similarly started, notably the specialized renaissance launched by John Wesley. Ingenious techniques, without The Spirit of God, resemble wood without fire; they produce neither warmth nor light. Yet techniques are good, when laid upon the altar. A Church consecrated to the Spirit, if Pentecost be taken seriously, will produce any number of spiritual, and material, resurrections. It is doubtful whether mere ingenuity of method can penetrate the consciences of men.

Turning from theology and evangelism to politics, Marc Boegner asserted that a social conscience was strong among French Christians. Both Protestants and Romans, for example, appointed ordained clergymen as ordinary laborers in French factories, to earn their bread by the sweat of their brows, to rub elbows and minds eight hours a day with working-men. French Protestantism, in particular, sought a balanced community-liberty regime which would avoid both totalitarian rigidity and egoistic anarchy. Christian charity had come to mean political as well as spiritual responsibility for one's neighbor. Almost without exception the theological Conservatives were the political Radicals, and the political Reactionaries the theological Liberals.

American Christians may take encouragement, and a score of workable ideas, from French Protestants, for their own heroic struggle to give the Free World and the Free Soul new moral strength, new spiritual depth, in man.

W. A. VISSER 'T HOOFT

It was one thing to go to Geneva, home of the Second Reformation, the World Council of Churches; it was another to find W. A. Visser 'T Hooft, its General Secretary. I had not been able to ascertain in advance the hour of my arrival; it had not been possible therefore to make an appointment. Visser 'T Hooft's thoughtful secretary, in the city made famous by John Calvin, phoned the

World Council Executive at the Chateau de Bossey, Celigny, Switzerland, and arranged a luncheon interview. After a few Kodachromes of Geneva's glories, I was on my way again.

The Ecumenical Institute at Celigny is part of the educational work of the World Council. Immensely to my surprise and pleasure, Hendrik Kraemer of the University of Leyden in Holland, along with Christian leaders from the ends of the Earth, was in attendance. When I read his book, *The Christian Message In A Non-Christian World,* several years ago, during the preparation of my doctoral dissertation, I never expected to see the beloved author in the flesh. He was kind enough to sit at my right at luncheon, while Visser 'T Hooft on my left considered my questions.

At the luncheon table, with Ecumenical leaders from the United States and Europe as well as from India and China and many another land, questions, answers, and courses were intermingled. Call it a gastronomic interview, if you like, but the custom of utilizing mealtime for partaking of the Bread of the Spirit is not a new one.

The World Council was not primarily interested in statistics, said Visser 'T Hooft, for the best statistics were fully as misleading as informing. One hundred and twelve Christian denominations were then enrolled as members from thirty-eight countries. (At last report the number has become one hundred ninety-two). No attempt had been made to estimate the number of Church-members thus represented. *Time* magazine, reporting from New Delhi, recently recorded the number, as we have seen, at 300,000,000.

The World Council, he said, did not consider itself in any sense an End, rather a Means for promoting the consciousness of basic unity among those "committed to faith in Christ as God and Saviour." The many, in the sharing of the defining Faith, were One. The World Council expressed this unity objectively, and around it provided fellowship in faith and practice. A common missionary enterprise was, and remains, a major development.

Certain geographical areas were not then represented. The Russian Orthodox Church had not entered the fellowship, though great hope existed that it would do so. Unitarian Societies, to preserve independence of mind, had not applied for membership. The Czechoslovakian Church, born with the State at the end of World War I, and in revolt against its former Roman domination, had expressed no interest. One of the last denominations to unite with the World Council had been the Armenian Nestorian Church of the Middle East.

I asked W. A. Visser 'T Hooft's opinion of E. Stanley Jones' idea — a United Church of America. A Federal Union was proposed in which each denomination would retain its identity in administration and ideology. Visser 'T Hooft saw no real advance in Jones' suggestion over the Federal Council of Churches of Christ in America. Basic in the World Council, he strongly affirmed, was the principle that unity of organization, not based on unity of commitment, only hindered real unity. A deep consciousness of oneness in Christ, not mere external uniformity, he said, was the objective of the World Council. If real unity existed around Christ's Kingship, despite secondary differences, in due time unity of organization might come into being. The patient, unhurried process could not be reversed. Physical unity could not precede unity of Mind and Spirit. Nominal uniformity, without spiritual community, he asserted, was a fundamental defect in Modern Protestantism.

Had the World Council defined its position, I enquired, concerning the third Person in Christianity's classical Trinity? W. A. Visser 'T Hooft explained that the doctrine of the Holy Spirit had been widely discussed, in particular at the sessions seeking to define the Christian Idea of the Church. However, the specific requirement of faith in the Holy Spirit had not been included in the World Council's statements.[1] No requirement had been included concerning faith in God the Father, not because the World Council was an organization of atheists, but because the definitive Trinitarian doctrine was the Deity of Christ. Faith in the Holy Spirit as

---

1. As C. S. Lewis once observed to me, "According to the Gospel of John, it is the work of the Holy Spirit to call attention not to himself but to Christ."

the Giver of Divine Life to finite human understanding was subsumed by all who believed "in Christ as God and Saviour." Member denominations did in fact believe in the Personality of the Holy Spirit, and in their dependence upon Him. The common desire had been to stress simplicity rather than complexity in printed statements of belief. The formula had been focused upon the Christian view of Christ because few men had ever believed in the Deity of Christ who were not Trinitarians. All the doctrines, he urged, were included in the one.

It was clear what the World Council regarded as "the essentials." What exactly, I asked, would be regarded as "the non-essentials"? Visser 'T Hooft replied that uniformity would never be sought on matters of Church Order — for example, on the proper number of genuflections as one approached the Altar. Some ideas of Church Government, however, were of more than passing importance — for example, that authority be given only to mature Christians. Similarly, since the World Council was in no sense Fundamentalist (Fundamentalism being largely of American origin), there would be no required unity of view concerning the precise manner of Biblical inspiration. Following the lead of Karl Barth and others, a great new awakening had taken place among Evangelicals. The necessity of "getting at" the Bible's essential message, and recognizing that message as God's Word to man, had been re-emphasized. This conviction had nothing in common with Fundamentalism's familiar Literalism; the World Council welcomed Higher Criticism's ground-clearing operations. The idea was a patient penetration to the actual Biblical message, its relevance to all modern men, the Word of God speaking through the Bible to the spiritually alert.

This apparently new emphasis in Protestantism, asserted Visser 'T Hooft, was, after all, but a renewal of the Reformation idea, that the Bible was not merely the word of man, to be lightly regarded, but in a profound sense the Word of God — speaking now in poetry misread as prose, or the reverse, but containing the definitive Christian foundation of growing World Community.

The Bible, he suggested, was not unlike the lofty peaks, rising out of lake and plain to vast heights, I had beheld on every side as I journeyed from Lausanne to Montana-sur-Sierre in the Swiss Alps. A man who has never seen the Great Hills must regard the little hills as large; a man who has never seen a Giant must look upon all Pigmies as giants. The little hills of France, so far behind, were like the lesser words of men. The Great Word has been spoken. It is our human part to seek spiritual discernment, to hear and obey the Divine message. The nuclear bomb is a great and terrible word of man, for or against human dignity and world community, but Alpine Hills seem unalarmed. The Word of God will survive the half-real or unreal words of men, and the great, explosive words of tyrants. Alexander, Genghis Khan, Napoleon, and Hitler were terrors for an hour, but are gone.

The main step toward the resurrection of Evangelical Protestantism, asserted Visser 'T Hooft, was the rediscovery of its original principle. For some generations Protestantism, faithless to its heritage, had wandered off after strange gods called Solipsism and Anarchy. Creative Protestantism was, from the beginning, a revolt from de-spiritualized Romanism to the Word of God. Modern Protestantism, he said, was without life-giving power in so far as it had become more deeply de-spiritualized than Rome ever was. With the rediscovery of the Word of God, Protestantism would return to health and vigor. Only upon the Rock of His Word could Christ re-build His Church. There was no other way to a living relation with the Holy Spirit, to "a live theology", to an effective Free World advance.

The shallow social gospel of feeble generations, Visser 'T Hooft continued, had recognized no Ultimate Power, no Voice of God commanding it to translate noble ideas into action. Liberalism had defended the Free Mind and the Free World, but underestimated the Voice of God, the Ultimate Command, with faith in Final Victory. It had no heart for the spiritual, social action which would not accept defeat. The Theology of Revelation did not *allow* a man to be socially responsible; it *required* in him a social conscience, would never let him rest with problems half solved. It summoned him to an all-out mobilization of the human best; it offered no comfortable compromise.

41

At this point I quoted Toynbee's declarations that Marxism had borrowed Ecumenicity and Humanitarianism from Christianity, without acknowledging the Source, but had left out the one thing needful to make the ideas work: the Ultimate Will requiring them, and the Ultimate Love quickening the human spirit into Life.

Barth and Brunner were, at one and the same time, enemies of Marxian materialism, and friends of Religious Socialism. They sought, said Visser 'T Hooft, to translate political into economic democracy, and rested the whole enterprise on the Word of God. Visser 'T Hooft confessed himself a Socialist in the same sense, and pointed to Hendrik Kraemer on my right as one of the moving spirits in Dutch Socialism, one of the founders of Holland's Labor Party. All men of like faith were unalterably opposed to totalitarian bureaucracy. Justice in society had to be constructed upon a Community Conscience, at the opposite extreme from coercive Collectivism.

HENDRIK KRAEMER

Some years ago, when I read Kraemer's stirring volume, *The Christian Message In A Non-Christian World,* I felt what is usually regarded as a childish impulse to write to the great man the keen appreciation awakened in me for the first and only book in recent years on the World Mission of Christianity which seemed fully aware of the nature, and dignity, of the other-than-Christian mind, to which the Christian must speak, with which he shares our common humanity. The volume of a generation ago, *Re-Thinking Missions,* of unquestioned nobility of purpose, was an original attempt to re-define Christianity, to reduce its distinctiveness, its identity and character, essential to its conversation, its fellowship, its communion with, and mission to, other moral religions. Christ was regarded as unique, in the local color of prophetic Judaism, but something less than the Incarnation of the Mind of God in the mind of man. The Christian Mission was to be re-designed as fellowship without creative difference, a superficial adventure in international friendship; it urged amalgam rather than meaning; troubled humanity. Even the notable two volumes by my friend, it was not at all a sacrificial mediation of an Ultimate Truth to

42

Edmund D. Soper (not closely related, but sharing same ancestral book, Washington, D.C.), while stressing admirably the uniqueness of Jesus, lacked in some measure the penetration, the startling rediscovery of the breakthrough of Reality, of an Absolute Invitation to human fellowship across difference, characteristic of Kraemer's book. The latter volume was the only one of its kind I had ever seen, or have yet seen, which seemed to capture the Christian message squarely — without which fellowship itself would be hypocrisy. The essential point, as I recall, was that all religions, including culture Christianity, were noble efforts on the part of spiritually thirsting humanity to reach up after God, whereas Christ represented the reverse movement, God reaching down to man, and, as such, represented also the Divine Answer to the human question, the Water of Life, qualitatively Eternal, to slake a world-wide thirst. The Christian missionary was, and is, no doubt an ambassador of international good will to Problem-ridden people, but also the bearer of the Solution for which, consciously or unconsciously, all men are reaching out. Clearly, this is the historic meaning of the Christian Mission, as understood by Matthew, Mark, and Luke, as well as by Peter, John, and Paul, and a host of martyrs in Rome. A mathematician can speak with, and to, all men — but he cannot make two plus two equal three or five, though he die for it.

I wrote this section, in first draft, within the crumbling walls of the Roman Coliseum, musing upon the blood there shed that tyranny might be destroyed and an everlasting Freedom-in-Fellowship erected; I could not but remember that to the martyrs Christ was the Infinite made Finite for human salvation, God above all other gods, Reality Itself, Truth Itself, Beauty Itself, established forever for all. No religious emphasis constructed upon a fragment of this Faith has full right to the name Christianity. The profound commitment of the martyrs gathered up the neglected glories of the extinct Hellenic Civilization, created our Western Society, our attempt to unite Freedom with Faithfulness. Without this Faith, as Toynbee has asserted, Western Civilization would substitute caricature for character.

43

You can perhaps understand that a private Doxology was singing in my soul as I sat with Hendrik Kraemer, after luncheon indoors and coffee under the trees, in a shaded part of the wide lawn at Chateau de Bossey, overlooking Lac Lamon. There questions were asked, and what I cannot but regard as more than relative answers were given.

The first and basic necessity for the resurrection of Evangelical Protestantism, said Hendrik Kraemer, was a true renewal of a life of prayer among all Christians, that a new upsurging of Christ's Spirit might be awakened in men. Until Life was restored from the Source of Life, with prayer and faith of deepened honesty, no real resurrection would be experienced. From the beginning Christianity had been a Breakthrough of Reality, a work of God, a Divine Labor in response to human need — at once an Evolution and a Revolution in Society and the Soul. Present Protestantism seemed both dead and deadening, said Kraemer, and would continue in its present state as long as pastors and people were under the impression that all building was the relative work of their own hands, at no point containing, or transmitting, the Grace of God.

Kraemer mentioned a letter he had recently received from a woman, a lay member of a Protestant Church, thanking him, as I had wanted to do, for his book, and describing her typical problem. She believed in Christ, sought in daily prayer the guidance of His Spirit, but was forced to recognize that what passed for Christianity at her Church seemed lifeless, unable either to interest or grip her growing sons and daughters.

Only a new baptism of Christ's Life and Spirit, which could come when men desired it with intense longing and sought it with hearts and minds, could make a thing "dead and deadening" live and breathe again, and draw men young and old with the proven charm of glowing vitality.

Without a quickened consciousness of the penetration of the Relative by the Absolute, human devices and techniques, and the best of human wisdom — admirable in themselves, demanding all-out support — would develop only change without progress, the "buzzing of chimera in the void."

44

The necessity of building the bridge from Christ to the Churches was first; second was an inevitable bridge-building from the Churches to the masses.

So significant did this insight seem to Hendrik Kraemer that he returned to it again and again throughout our conversation. What the Church needed most was Life and Power, an increase of the Absolute in the Relative. The Church had numbers, wealth, prestige; it needed only Vitality, Reality, Vigor from Above. On this point Kraemer had but recently written a message to postwar Christians, urging them to give themselves once again in dead earnest to God, beseeching Him for the gift of Christ's Mind for altar fire to set ablaze the human kindling.

At point two in Kraemer's discussion of Protestant needs, the emphasis was practical as well as spiritual. Precisely speaking, the second need of Evangelical Protestantism, he said, was to invent or acquire a vocabulary that modern pagans, in or out of Churches, might comprehend. The language of theological leadership, for obvious reasons, had been the specialized dialect of University and Seminary, not the everyday speech of the people. When the most ardent emissary of the Gospel harangued common folk, there was little possibility of their understanding him. The most important bridge that had to be constructed by the genius of Christian charity was the bridge of words, of symbols, of speech, for was not language invented as a means of communication? The Seminaries in particular had to shake off antiquated speech, let the clean breeze of the Gospel sweep across the mind. Not till then would the Miracle, the more than relative Life, become the Thrill and Thrust of the masses.

I reminded Kraemer that Barth had agreed with the Pauline declaration that the natural man could not understand the things of the Spirit. I mentioned Emil Brunner's alternate emphasis that the capacity to receive the Gospel existed in the depraved. Kraemer considered both viewpoints true. On the one hand, a human being, darkened by egoism and lust, could have but little, or hidden, spiritual discernment. Only as the Great Light dawned in the darkened mind could the mind itself penetrate deeply the innocent and the holy. Nevertheless a basic commandment had been to preach the Gospel to every creature; there would have been no point in the Word if there were nothing in the hearts and minds of men to receive it. Something in the most depraved of men was not unresponsive to the True Word, the True Deed, of True Love. In any case, our opinion had not been sought on the issue. Rather a clear command had been given. If we were obedient, we would declare the Word, with the calm assurance that no Good Seed is ever sown in vain; with our effort, our sacrifice, our charity, the Gospel would be heard and understood.

Any kind of bridge-building from the Gospel to the Common Mind was of the Lord, he said. He cited "the Christian Commando" movement, a united effort in personal Evangelism among London Churches. Such a movement, while not sufficient in itself, was in the right direction — the direction John Wesley traveled; in his travail of spirit and flesh a measure of New Life was born. Woodrow Wilson, it will be remembered, made the same point when, as President of Princeton University, he declared in repeated lectures about the nation that the Wesleys had saved England from the madness of the French Revolution.

In this matter as in others the Will would find the Way; a firm resolve in Churchmen, "to make the Gospel known among the people," would not fall short of its goal.

In this discussion of practical means for reaching the masses, Kraemer returned with emphasis to the main theme. The first step, in practical Evangelism, was the recognition that, of ourselves, "we were *not* able" to build the bridge. God had already built it; we ourselves were the bridge to the people, for we ourselves were people. Nonetheless, a false belief in our own sufficiency had brought the Church to its partial Rigor Mortis. It was hard for the average man, perhaps, to see that two things, seemingly contradictory, were required: 1 — to realize that "of himself he could do nothing"; and 2 — to give his energy and intelligence to practical effort. Something more, and older, than a man could then work through him, an ageless idea — as Aristotle understood. Yesterday it may have been true that men realized their helplessness without the Seed-receiving and Seed-growing Soil, but they sometimes neglected to go forth with songs to the sowing. They waited for God to do everything. They were right in looking to God for the harvest, wrong in not obeying His specific command to labor till the setting of the sun. More recently the reverse seemed the popular disobedience: men were full of labor, busy with devices and techniques, not unlike the French Army in the spring of 1940, but their labor and their ingenuity were without the wonder-working Power. Both halves of the Truth were necessities: we were required to trust and pray as though *all* depended upon God, as it did indeed; at the same time we were required to labor as though *all* depended upon us, as in a secondary way it did also.

At one extreme men were crying, "Lord, Lord," but not "doing the will of the Father in Heaven"; at the other, men were crying, "Lord, Lord," in a different way, and were differently, yet similarly too, "not doing the Father's will." The two elements, trust and obedience, held together, were undefeatable; apart, neither had the gift of Life — in work or in war.

It was not to be understood that practical Evangelism could evade in any fashion its intellectual responsibility, as to a large extent it had tended to do. The first requirement of Evangelism was to understand deeply and usably the Creative Word of the Christian. How could any evangelist, however gifted, put across an idea unknown to him? Much of the recent stagnation in Christendom had come about because zealous evangels had been strong in purpose but feeble in power and process, in comprehension of the message they were commanded to deliver. Like Ahimahaz in the army of Joab, gifted with long legs but a numb skull, first to arrive at David's tent but without the message to be delivered, much modern Evangelism had developed great speed but forgotten the purpose of the errand. Like the early pseudo-scientists, Evangelism had endeavored at times by an unchristian *alchemy* to change intellectual stultification into virtue. A patient mastery of the Gospel, a thorough comprehension of its point, was a clear necessity if a message worth hearing were to reach the people. I outlined Emil Brunner's emphasis on "a live theology." The purpose of Evangelism would be defeated if the Christian centralities remained the exclusive possession of the clergy. If the Gospel

47

were to shrink into a monopoly of ecclesiastics, great harm would be done, had already been done. It was required that parents teach Christianity to their children, teachers to their pupils, laymen to one another and the man in the street.

Professor Kraemer, permanent Director of the World Council's Institute Ecumenique at Celigny, came thus to his last point. It was necessary that there be a world-wide recovery of the original Protestant idea — the direct and immediate Priesthood of every Believer. On this Rock Protestantism had been built; any other foundation would prove shifting sand. Professionalism in an age afflicted with "a division of labor" had crept, like a cancer, into the Body of Christ, had thwarted and frustrated the labor of the Lord. A Church was an organism, not an organization; it lived in every cell, or in none. On this subject I called attention to the identity between Kraemer's emphasis and the Barthian idea that true Evangelism was an affair of the entire "Community of Christ." Unless laymen, Christians by conviction, labored together with the Lord, the pastor would be a shepherd of pagan sheep; as pastors and priests have sometimes been, he would be a mere link between the pagan congregation and Christianity, a nostalgic symbol of the forgotten reason for the Church's existence.

One might conclude from all this that Hendrik Kraemer was onesided in his thinking — all otherworldliness, no tension with the concrete problems of external society. This conclusion, however, would be strikingly erroneous, for when our discussion moved from the needs of the Church to the needs of the State, the Prophet of Leyden proved no less relevant. America, he said, with its vast resources, only beginning to be developed, could possibly afford the luxury of enterprise completely free, of rugged and rough individualism, of economic anarchy, without the total submergence of the underprivileged. However, anyone who lived in postwar Europe, with its limited resources, could see at a glance that an unplanned economy was too costly a luxury. Christianity had lived under all kinds of political and economic regimes, because it was not a means to a political end, but an avenue of God to men; yet Christians, in whom Charity truly lived, could not but see that an awakened conscience and a lawless economy could not, like the lion and the lamb, lie down peaceably together.

Christianity, asserted Kraemer, had no common ground with Marxian materialism as a philosophy, yet might find its own external objectives best realized in a practical Socialism. Christianity, in its social aspect, sought finally one thing — a solution to public problems by the mobilization of the available best in men and material, yet insisted at the same time on the protection of minorities and the rights of individuals. The common interest had to take precedence over even sacred private property. Christianity was realistic; it simply sought to solve problems. Because it was conscious always of the individual as the only link between society and God, it was inevitably neutral about political and economic systems *in themselves.* It asked only: "Which one, while preserving spiritual freedom, will best do the job needing to be done?" If Socialism offered the most realistic solution to specific social problems, Christianity would automatically be forced to vote Socialist, he said, conscious of the dangers to faith and liberty, yet seeking honest solutions to real problems with a politically unprejudiced mind.

With a deep sense of economic responsibility, Kraemer had taken a leading part in the organization of the Dutch Labor Party. Objectives included nationalization of basic industries, universal hospital insurance, high labor standards, public-spirited action to improve the lot of peasants and factory-workers, and the independence of Dutch Borneo. The Labor Party had been formed with the specific understanding that liberty of religion and of speech were to be preserved, that the Church, not to be attacked by the Party, was rather to be acknowledged as receiving its Life from God, to be recognized also as the People's Ally and Champion in every righteous cause. Not the totalitarian tyranny of Bolshevism, intent upon the shedding of blood not its own, but the Christian Community seeking common solutions to common problems under the inspiration, and criticism, of the Church — this was the programme of the Dutch Labor Party, to which Kraemer, precisely because he was a Christian, was committed.

There was an unstudied humility, the selflessness of piety and charity, shining out of Hendrik Kraemer's personality. Here in one original, profound mind, the supersensory and the sensory worlds had come into the perfect tension of mutual respect so familiar in the Sermon on the Mount: "Seek first the Kingdom of God; . . .these things shall be added unto you."

AMSTERDAM PERSONALITIES

Among memorable interviews at the Amsterdam Assembly, to New Delhi as Nicea was to Chalcydon, three in particular reflected, directly or by implication, the diversity which accompanies the unity of the Free World Mind.

While John Foster Dulles extolled Western law and freedom, and Joseph L. Hromadka, following Dulles, extolled Eastern economic equality, I gave my attention privately to Charles P. Taft, then chairman of the Federal Council of Churches of Christ in America. I had read the Dulles and Hromadka speeches in the press room earlier in the day; with easy conscience, therefore, I devoted my thought to a splendid American.

Taft had presided at the annual session in New York of the American Committee for the World Council of Churches, which I addressed. I was anxious to probe further his American mentality on three issues — his attitude toward rumored action to reduce the "Christ as God and Saviour" commitment of the World Council, his view, as brother of the American Senator, of the East-West economic conflict, and, finally, his analysis of his own story as a Christian.

It had not been a simple matter to arrange the hour. Two appointments had been made and broken by understandable complexities. I had experienced less trouble interviewing Jacques Maritain, French Ambassador to the Vatican, and Arnold J. Toynbee, prince of Ecumenical historians. I was aware of the World Assembly's strenuous pace, and profoundly grateful for the time at length given to my questions. I would not have pursued the conversation but for Taft's earlier statement that Assembly personalities would welcome interviews.

He was convinced, he said, that the World Council's present Christology would not be altered. A minority, from America and Switzerland, desired to modify the "God and Saviour" formula. Modification in the Unitarian direction, in his opinion, could not expect success. An effort to enlarge the present commitment might go through. The reception accorded the addresses of Barth and Dodd made it clear that the weight of the Assembly was interested only in a Divine human Christ. It was felt in many quarters, nonetheless, that the Humanity as well as the Deity of Christ needed accent. For himself, said Taft, he would prefer the "Divine Lord and Saviour" formula of the Federal Council.

He acknowledged, as a layman, that he was not a trained theologian, that his knowledge of theology had been gained almost wholly from the World Assembly itself. I asked, "Do you feel that theology should remain exclusively a clerical interest?" "No," he replied, "but I think the ancient creedal formulas, composed of Greek philosophy and Mediaeval Scholasticism, need translation into modern speech." I reported that this opinion had been expressed to me by Marc Boegner and Hendrik Kraemer.

I explained that I saw no harm in the "Divine Lord and Saviour" formula, provided that the word "Divine" was taken seriously, as the penetration of the finite by the Infinite, of the relative by the Absolute, rather than, as had often happened, as an adjective of mere admiration, the equivalent of "noble" or "highminded". The present formula, "God and Saviour," I suggested, had been adopted to outlaw, even as a possibility, the surrender of a point of Finality in the Christian Faith. Member Communions of the World Council, I urged, were in attendance because the present wording represented their serious commitment — in no sense their desire to exclude from their fellowship free minds from any part of the Free World.

Mr. Taft did not believe that Assembly exponents of Eastern or Western economics would be able to compose their differences in ten days. Much more important, he felt certain, was their common endeavor to consider the economic issue, not for the purpose of working out a neutral formula, but rather with a view to assisting actual individuals, under all economic systems, to maintain, or regain, their social and personal freedom. Such an effort might fail to establish a compromise economic philosophy, might indeed suffer from an excess of immediacy, yet in the long run prove most realistic in theory and most helpful in practice. He could go along, he said, with Hromadka's outline of the dangers in Eastern Economics, but could see only the familiar "Moscow line" in Hromadka's list of Communist virtues. Hromadka, in Taft's opinion, had accurately analyzed the hazards of totalitarian Communism, but had not emphasized them in his later statements.

His own biography as a Christian, said Taft, had been neither unique nor complicated. His great grandparents, on both sides, had been devoutly religious, at one wing Presbyterian, at the other Baptist. Presbyterianism had generally prevailed in the family's history, though his father had been a Unitarian. In Cincinnati he had attended the nearby Christ Church (Episcopal) Sunday School. He had learned the Catechism, but its good theology had not gone through his mental processes. Later in Washington he had been associated for many years with the YMCA, and at Northfield, Massachusetts, with the leadership of John R. Mott. He had always felt, however, that Mott's emphasis upon personal conversion, as emotional experience, had been unacceptable to modern youth.

Following the Taft interview, I talked briefly with the Tass Agency Reporter, George Afrin, assigned to cover the Assembly for Russian newspapers. Fate conspired to shorten our conversation. Two ideas, I suggested, had so far been expressed which Russia could approve — in part: Karl Barth's assertion that no identity, except in their mutual insistence upon freedom, could be assumed between Christianity and Capitalism; and second, Hromadka's vigorous support of Eastern economic purpose. Afrin agreed, smiling, that these were wholesome items; he would certainly report them to Moscow. He asked me, "Do you think Wallace will be elected as the next American President?" I replied: "Not without Russian methods of armed coercion!" Afrin grinned broadly. I continued: "You see, in the States, the voters are privileged to choose between alternate parties; they are free to cast their ballots for the party they believe will best represent their interests." Afrin again smiled, and said: "In Russia we do not need two parties; one party meets all our needs." Afrin agreed with my statement that Amsterdam was a wonderful place to live. I was thinking of silent, apprehensive Prague, with its empty stores, and of Amsterdam's happy crowds and heavily laden shops. Afrin mumbled something about an appointment, and departed.

The third interview was, to me, the most meaningful. In America I had known Elmer L. Homrighausen of Princeton only through his excellent book, *Let the Church Be the Church.* I knew that he had been loaned for a period to the World Council office at Geneva. There were, he said, three clearly-defined groups at the Amsterdam Assembly. The major group, fortunately in actual leadership, possessed, in his opinion, both nominal belief in the Deity of Christ and Existential Faith, that is, personal experience of inward Grace. This group, he believed, constituted the "holy remnant," the Church within the Church, at the Convocation. A second group stoutly defended the creedal formula "Christ as God and Saviour," but, in his opinion, clearly did not have and did not value Existential Faith, inward Life in the Holy Spirit. This group would always have to be considered. Members of the third group assented to World Council Christology with their tongues in their cheeks, for they did not seriously believe in the transnatural Christ of universal Christian experience, nor did they possess spiritual vitality. This faction would always be a drag upon Ecumenical Christianity, for it would confuse the real issues, and regard the Assembly itself as of greater importance than Christ. Homrighausen was particularly appreciative of Barth's forceful reminder that the World Council was not God, though it might be His servant.

On the theme of economics, Homrighausen was convinced, the Assembly, without exception, believed in the economic brotherhood of man, yet, also without exception, disbelieved in Russian totalitarianism. Hromadka clearly saw the new Czech regime only in the ideal, as one of its leaders and spokesmen, as a personality approved by Moscow, not as one who knew by personal experience the Communist bureaucracy and its secret police surveillance, from the standpoint of the people, and not as its serious critic. Sooner or later, he would have to choose martyrdom or hypocrisy. He was, nonetheless, a most charming personality, and, to all appearances, though subject with all men to a notable lack of omniscience, thoroughly sincere.

Homrighausen is a gracious Christian personality indeed, and I felt a profound admiration for him. I am convinced that his analysis of the World Council was true. The façade of ecumenical harmony covered important differences, in theology as in economics, yet the unmistakable majority was committed to the Christ whom Christians recognize as Ancient Atonement and Contemporary Saviour; the same majority similarly championed political freedom as well as economic brotherhood.

In the evening near my hotel, as I watched Amsterdam's million canal lights come on in prevue of Queen Wilhelmina's Jubilee, an English youth on holiday accosted me. In a lengthy conversation at a side-walk cafe the youth stressed his bewilderment that he had been born into a nightmare universe of huge, political, economic, and religious machines, in which human beings lost all individuality, were considered mere anonymous cogs. The adults he knew seemed to seek only bread and power. He agreed, however, that at any moment and from any country the individual might lift his eyes and find himself no longer a robot idolator pursuing bread and power, no longer an anonymous cog in a vast machine, but a soul individually produced, sustained, and beloved by the Lord of all.

THE SWISS REFORMED POINT OF VIEW

CHRISTOPH BARTH

Many have heard of the father; few have heard of the son. The Theology of Revelation is considered otherworldly and impractical, at least among secularists, yet Karl Barth has imparted to his distinguished son a thorough grasp of essential Barthianism. Sons of great fathers often rebel against a mature judgment they do not understand, or consider their own bid for fame and fortune hopelessly overshadowed. Not so Christoph Barth, who has received the degree of Doctor of Theology in his own right, has been his father's constant collaborator, and was then to leave within the year to begin his chosen career as missionary at the Basel Sending, Dutch Borneo, Indonesia.

I was at first disappointed that Karl Barth, who startled the Protestant world in 1918 with his rediscovery of God, was at the moment beyond my reach, lecturing for the summer at the University of Bonn. Uncle Sam then firmly refused to allow me to visit Bonn, under the justifiable impression, no doubt, that Germany had troubles enough without the additional affliction of peripatetic Americans. I seemed to be holding a bag from which the treasure had vanished. However, careful investigation disclosed that it was not a bag I held in my hand but a magnifying glass, for Karl Barth's own work-room, with all his books, was open to me; available also, as guide, philosopher, and friend, was the best possible interpreter, the great man's companion, disciple, and son, Christoph.

I almost missed Christoph. Unable to locate Karl Barth either at his home or at the University of Basle, I directed my patient taxi-driver to the home of Karl Barth's friend, D. Edouard Tourneysen, also of Basle's theological faculty. I had been urged to visit Edouard Tourneysen by Marc Boegner in Paris, for Tourneysen's book on Dostoyevsky, not available in English, had attracted considerable attention on the continent. With the gracious Mrs. Tourneysen as hostess and interpreter, the Professor and I discussed eagerly our common interest, the great Russian. However, though our conversation was ostensibly on Dostoyevsky, I found Edouard and Mrs. Tourneysen avenues of advance into the mind of Karl Barth.

I was impressed by the fact, stressed by Professor Tourneysen, that both Karl Barth and himself, despite their alleged otherworldliness, had voted for the Socialist Party in control of the Basle Government. It would not be accurate to say that Karl Barth had uniformly espoused the cause of Swiss Socialism, asserted the Tourneysens, for he had rather considered each issue on its merits, evaluating the alternatives. In the main his support had been given to every Socialist effort to improve the material lot of workers and farmers, insofar as social legislation, in his opinion, could serve the purpose. Later in the morning Christoph Barth explained that in early days his father had vigorously supported the Socialist movement, then a religious as well as a political enterprise. He looked with suspicion on secular socialism, but examined specific issues as they confronted the people. He often voted alongside even the secular socialists, when it seemed to him that their program was realistic. With his photograph now before me, gift of the thoughtful Christoph, I can well understand the father's habit of weighing issues, theological or political, on their merits, and quite without the distortion of sentimentality. He looks as a prophet ought to look, with unruly hair and piercing eyes, yet with inner tranquility.

Professor Tourneysen emphasized two elements necessary to Protestant advance: first, a new relevance in preaching, with greater though not slavish use of the Bible; and second, an all-out drive to transfigure the *whole* of life, social and personal, with Divine Grace.

Mrs. Tourneysen urged that I see Christoph Barth, and it was she who made the appointment on my behalf.

56

Seated in one of the two rooms which constitute Karl Barth's private study, surrounded by his own almost innumerable volumes, with his remarkable collection of American and English mystery novels near at hand, his pipe and tobacco lying on the desk, his son across a circular coffee table from me, I felt the man himself not far away.

The simplest definition of Karl Barth's theology, asserted Christoph, was its proper title: the Theology of Revelation. "God speaks, and man hears." But the Bible was not itself the Word of God. Barth was damned as roundly by the Fundamentalists as by the Relativists. Rather Christ spoke to us through the Bible. We could not hear what He said by simply reading the Bible. Only the reading enlightened by an inward operation of the Holy Spirit enabled one to hear the Word of God. Only the same inward strengthening enabled a man to obey the Divine Command in the total reconstruction of social and personal life.

It had been falsely alleged by numerous opponents, said Christoph, that the Barthian emphasis relieved man of responsibility. I mentioned that on the Atlantic crossing it had been repeatedly asserted with gestures, indeed with all the assurance and enthusiasm which frequently accompany the lack of information, that Barthianism was an exceedingly dangerous movement, for young men trained in the tradition went forth to their ministry with but one conviction, that they must suspend all activity and await Divine intervention.

Christoph Barth was quick to declare that no one who had read his father's books could say that he preached a gospel of inaction. Man tended to build only upon shifting sand, when he built, with neither freedom nor fellowship, upon something less than the Word made flesh in Christ, upon a human mixture of evil with good. All permanent building is based, he said, not upon egoism and lust, but upon the Divine Word. And the Divine Word did not exempt men from activity, from possible sacrifice and martyrdom, but rather required a redemptive activity both inward and social.

To say that the Theology of Revelation advocated human inaction, or human exemption from responsibility, aside from the abysmal lack of knowledge displayed by the statement, was simply to say that there was no Divine Word. If Christ the Word had spoken to men, the obedience which He required involved a total activity of an intense kind, from the beginning to the end of every phase of life.

During the last Great War, asserted Christoph, the practical worth of his father's messages to the French people, in the building of morale and the strengthening of resistance, had been immeasurable, and everywhere recognized. They must resist Hitler to the death in the name of Christ, Karl Barth had urged, lest in addition to their land they surrender also their souls. When Roman leaders were collaborating with the Petain government, and only Pacifist voices could be heard among Protestants, Karl Barth's writing proved "a trumpet with a certain sound" to heroic French Christians, giving them heart in a difficult hour. Had not this been a practical Gospel? It had summoned the French to realistic resistance to evil in the name of God.

In Holland, the theological Liberals had proven political Obstructionists, opposing the liberation of Borneo, while theological Conservatives had shown themselves political Liberals. The extreme Fundamentalists had demonstrated their indifference to social questions, as was to be expected, for they considered religion and government two irreconcilable worlds, and were themselves from the wealthy classes. The Evangelicals or Barthians, as Christoph had witnessed, had continuously supported a thoroughgoing application of Christian ethics in Dutch politics.

A second false attack had alleged that Karl Barth taught a selfish or purely individualist salvation. Again the critics had been misinformed, said Christoph. Barth emphasized the significance of individual personality, as did any non-collectivist thinker, but even more stressed the concept of the Church. The Community of Christ had always preceded the mere preaching of an individual Gospel. The preaching was important, but not as important as the witness of the entire Christian Community, composed of Christians-by-conviction who took Christ with them into the whole of life. The hope of the world was the kind of leadership not elsewhere available than in the Community of Christ, presenting its Divine summons to spiritual and social resurrection.

This emphasis, I pointed out, was identical with Nicholas Berdiaeff's distinction between Collectivism and Community, the former a mechanical organization, a Frankenstein monster, maintained exclusively by force, the latter an organism set in motion by a fellowship of kindred minds. Without the leadership of the living Church, the Body of Christ, composed of disciples by conviction and love, what could mankind do but, as sheep without the True Shepherd, obey the false shepherd through fear of physical violence, or faint and be scattered abroad?

The message of Karl Barth, summoning the living Church to hear and obey Christ the Word, said Christoph, was primarily a social Gospel, though, to be sure, not the pseudo-social gospel which was secularism clothed in sacraments. The Barthian social Gospel was not secular at all, but both spiritual and practical, heeding the supersensory Voice in a sensory world.

It was clear, as we talked, that the Church could not consciously hear a supersensory Voice it did not acknowledge. A Church which had substituted sociology for theology obviously could not base its activity on an Ultimate Word it regarded as unspoken. Hence, the first necessity, he said, if the Church was to be Christ's Witness in the world, was for Churchmen to listen to the Voice of Christ as God and Saviour. Then, and then only, would the resurrection of Evangelical Protestantism take place — when the Church heard, when the Church obeyed.

One might enquire, upon reflection, why this-worldly Protestants, not exclusively secular, have so wholeheartedly damned Karl Barth as otherworldly? Perhaps the dual nature of classical Christianity is the clue. Christianity begins with a Christ both God and Man, continues in a Church both Divine and Human, speaks in a Bible both Eternal and Temporal, baptizes faulty human personalities with the faultless Holy Spirit, and evokes justice in society from half-just men. The myopia which sees the human but not the Divine, the relative but not the Absolute, in Christ, in the Church, in the Bible, in the Christian, in the State, must always regard as otherworldly the vision less blind.

C. S. Lewis found, during his early years of unbelief, that in essentials all Christians shared a common Faith. There were differences, to be sure, some of more than superficial significance, for St. Francis of Assisi was a Roman while John Wesley was an Anglican, Augustine was an ancient while George Macdonald was a modern, Luther was a German while Calvin was a Frenchman, and so forth endlessly. About them all, however, there was a common atmosphere, distasteful in the extreme to a self-satisfied agnostic. The outsider, for his own justification, might try, but could not drive any fundamental wedge between Christians. The lines Christians drew between themselves were important but secondary.

Christian students, who have read both Barth and Brunner, for example, are able to point out real and not at all imaginary differences. Between Paul and Barnabas there were sharp differences which their common biographer, Luke, made no attempt to write down. Yet one Christ, as crucified and risen God and Saviour, was proclaimed by both to the end of their days, to the conversion of multitudes, and to their own martyrdom. The Christian Church, the Community of Christ, it seems, resembles in this regard a great mediaeval Cathedral, constructed in love and faith by multitudes of anonymous workers over many generations. Mentalities differ, and personalities vary, yet "him that cometh unto Me I will in no wise cast out." There is no room at all in the Kingdom of Heaven for idlers, onlookers, by-standers, but all the room in the world for workers committed to Christ, whatever their secondary differences.

Emil Brunner's conception of the basic divergence between Barth and himself was first among my questions from the happy moment when, finding the sage of Zurich at home with his wife and son, I accepted the heartening coffee and began our interview. The actual asking of the question came last in time, for other issues were important as well, and one hesitates to begin an interview by waving a controversial flag.

Though we did not discuss the Barth-Brunner divergence till later, Emil Brunner himself raised the issue in passing as we approached another theme. He said, "I suppose from America Barth and I must look a good deal alike." "Yes," I replied. "You are both suspected by Americans of believing in a God Who is more than a name." Brunner was amused at my description of a group of students and professors at Beloit which we christened "The Heretics", organized by our Department of Religion, who share what G. K. Chesterton called "the modern heresy" of believing that Christ was and is "God with us."

Marc Boegner, at our interview in Paris, had characterized as "soup" the pan-religious relativism represented by the well-meaning organization called the World Alliance for Friendship between the Churches, which had attempted to bring representatives of all religions into "spatial adjacency" around the collected absence of a common commitment to a diversely translatable Ultimate, the Brahman in the Atman, if you like, for western religion its faith in Christ as God and Saviour. The World Council of Churches, on the other hand, had already played its practical role in creating an atmosphere under which diverse Christian denominations had actually come together, subordinating secondary differences. I reported this part of the Boegner interview for Brunner's comment.

Among European Christian leaders, said Emil Brunner, there was no disagreement about faith in Christ as God and Saviour as the true basis of Ecumenicity. In all the discussions looking toward the World Conference at Amsterdam, for example, this defining commitment had remained uppermost. Some American representatives to these gatherings had appeared alarmed at this confirmation of "modern heresy", but, being a minority, had been powerless to claim the World Council for Relativism, and, despite the American tendency to lag behind continental theology, had possibly carried back to the States an echo of universal Christianity. Not all American Seminaries had bowed the knee to the Baal of Relativism, notably Princeton and Drew; there were signs of resurrection everywhere, including the University of Chicago. While there was life, even a diverse life, in American Protestantism, there was also hope.

Only one thing could regenerate American Protestantism, said Emil Brunner — "a live theology." Around the presence of an Idea of the Absolute any movement could grow, but a Protestantism which de-spiritualized its classical heritage for imagined modern palates could have no future. The provincial American desire to escape Christian theology had simply produced an incoherent theology. Any effort to get along without the *use* of the Free Mind would prove a shortlived enterprise at best. Christianity was not merely a lovable religion; it was also both thinkable and livable. When any part of it was missing, it limped along like a cripple. Christianity had always gone into decline when it neglected its basic Ideas. Protestantism in the United States had prestige, the prestige of an established religion; it had also money, numbers, and power; it had, as well, the diseases and dangers of success — *avoirdupois,* hardening of the arteries, shortness of breath, and heart trouble. In fact, American Protestantism suffered most from an old disease, Respectability. In the midst of Prosperity, earned by the sweat of earlier brows, there was danger of laying aside the Faith which had mobilized the original power and created Prosperity. The first necessity was the recovery of the Christian Faith. It was even possible that it was merely mislaid, not wholly lost. There were many signs that Christianity still existed in American Protestantism, neither hardened into Fundamentalism nor softened into Relativism. There was nothing in the situation which "a live theology", touched into energy by the Spirit of God, would not cure.

Improved "techniques" of Evangelism, while helpful, could not take the place of "a live theology." Only Life could win either admirers or disciples. No one could be persuaded by devices, however ingenious, to subscribe to a dead idea, or to climb aboard a sinking ship.

I was reminded of Kierkegaard's prayer: "O Holy Spirit, take away the power of mastery, and give us life."

Only ideas have given life to things, asserted Emil Brunner, and for nineteen centuries, where the Christian Ideas have been known, they have exalted whole societies. At the moment the world was athirst, like a parched land, for the Water of Life, simply because the Great Idea had been lost to view. What regenerating power remained existed because the Gospel had been preached, had possessed lives, had won the nations by its charm. Only charm would win disciples, and the recovery of Christianity's "live theology," its historic Idea, could alone create the charm.

Brunner was in agreement with Niebuhr that classical Christianity had to be rescued from the Nessus shirt of Fundamentalism. Literalists held the Word of Life in a context of distortion. However, with Boegner and Berdiaeff, Brunner was convinced that in the latter part of the nineteenth century Christian leaders, with naive capitulation to an elsewhere valid scientific method, had established a dishonorable rapport with essential science, usually misunderstood, through the surrender of "a live theology." The theological illiteracy, which had resulted from an exclusive preoccupation with sensory science, had contributed only to confusion, not to the resurrection of the Divine Image in man.

In Brunner's opinion, Christianity existed *in* the world; Christ's witnesses had to understand the world to which they mediated the Light of Faith. However, he said, when Christians forgot that Christianity was not *of* the world, the Church proved powerless to transfigure society or to transform earth-dwellers, by the renewing of their minds, the growth of their social and personal freedom, into citizens of the City of God.

I pointed out that Toynbee had similarly described the sorrow which visited the creative minority when, in its anxiety to transform society by the direct influence of spirit upon spirit and by the use of *mimesis* or social drill, it lost its creative idea and succumbed to the world it sought to redeem. Unless the Church recovered its creative Idea, that the Absolute in Person had entered into Time, it would become indistinguishable from the Civilization to which it was sent on the errand of the Lord.

I enquired whether Emil Brunner had any suggestions concerning the best sequence in reading his books. He regarded the books on Ethics as distinct from, though not unrelated to, the volumes on Philosophy and Theology. One might read the latter in the following order: *The Divine-Human Encounter, Revelation and Reason,* and *The Mediator* — all available. The best of the volumes on Ethics, he said, would probably be *The Divine Imperative.*

What might be considered the proper relation between Christianity and politics? I asked. In Brunner's view, the Christian might experiment with Socialism, for he would take seriously the Divine Word summoning him to total responsibility for the well-being of the human family; he would favor the mobilization of group resources for the solution of group problems. The Christian, however, could not enter the Closed Communion of the Communists, for he did not agree with Marxist philosophers that man could live by bread alone. The Christian was unalterably opposed to Collectivism with its annihilation of the individual and its deification of the state, with its denial of matters spiritual and its exclusive preoccupation with matters mechanical, its apparent failure to recognize that Communism itself, in Idea, is nonmaterial. The Christian was as strongly opposed to the western misuse of the glorious word, Liberty, which sometimes degraded it to license, solipsism, relativism, and anarchy. The Church, the creative minority of the Lord, was the Divine-Human Community, able, when truly alive and wholly itself, to make of society a family. Brunner was greatly interested that Berdiaeff was then at work on a book developing a similar idea.

Emil Brunner's gracious wife, who supplied me repeatedly with the best coffee I had tasted in Europe, and his brilliant son, Hans Henry Brunner, Graduate of Union Seminary in New York and newly appointed Professor of the Philosophy of Religion at Wellesley College, Massachusetts, were deeply amused when eventually I asked the Zurich philosopher: "How would you describe the basic divergence between Barth and yourself?" I acknowledged that this must be a tiresome question, since the main disagreement was not a new one. Hans Henry Brunner smiled and said, "This must be the thousandth time." Emil Brunner was patient and generous in his answer: "The difference is that Barth thinks as a Churchman, while I think as a Missionary. He writes as though his readers understood a Christian vocabulary. I write as though my readers were pagans. Barth believes that the secular mind cannot possibly understand a Christian idea; I believe that, by virtue of membership in God's world, by virtue of being a Divine creation, however disfigured, every man has within himself, whether pagan or Christian, something to which the Gospel, a live theology, may directly appeal."

THE ANGLICAN POINT OF VIEW

C. S. LEWIS

I had not elsewhere experienced the high tension of spirit C. S. Lewis evoked in me. There was keenness of anticipation, as I approached his rooms, and the joy of high discovery, like the rejoicing of the man in Christ's parable who found "treasure hid in a field"; there was breathlessness, excitement of mind. For C. S. Lewis is not quite like other writers. Ability to stimulate sustained thought on the great topics seems abnormally concentrated in him. There are other commanding generals in the Army of the Lord; they have made inestimable contributions to thinking Christians. But C. S. Lewis is different; you find yourself using his ideas and forgetting that they are his. His mind seems a colossal picture-making machine, and each picture reduces a great and terrible theological abstraction to the clarity of a Gospel parable. He moves in on you, and possesses the stray ends of your imagination, not by the color and fire of his intellectual pyrotechnics, as his enemies assert, but rather by the simple reality of his service to your spirit. He answers your questions, and fills in the open spaces between your ideas. Yet, while he is a necessary supplement to the diet of an advanced thinker (Etienne Gilson showed me the Lewis volumes on his shelves and expressed his joy in them), you can really give him to children. I have toyed, at times, with the idea of a learned essay on his central conceptions, and I may yet give in to the temptation, for good or ill, but truly he is himself so much more readable, interesting, and profitable, than anything, particularly than any ponderous scholarly analysis, that could be written about him. *Apostle to the Skeptics,* by my Beloit friend Chad Walsh, is the best Lewis treatment I have seen. The Lewis books fulfill one requirement of great classics; they are uniformly more gripping than the secondary sources. And if his major influence, George Macdonald, about whom he has written as affectionately as Plato wrote about Socrates, had half his own spiritual discernment and sparkle of imagination, he was truly a man for the ages.

As I entered his rooms at Magdalene College (pronounced Maudlin), he was smiling with light in his soul. He seated me opposite him, and enquired whether there was too much draft from the open window. He said, "I do hope you are not feeling, as one of your countrymen did recently, upon seeing me for the first time, when he said, 'I am disappointed in you,' and then repeated it." I confessed that my reaction was quite the reverse. He looked exactly as I had pictured him; I was pleased in every way with what I saw. Oxford acquaintances had described to me his normal apparel — unmatched coat and trousers. He had once addressed a congregation at Oxford's Wesley Memorial Chapel attired in lounge coat, slacks, and tennis shoes. Clothing, it appeared, was to him a secondary matter, not to be given undue attention. The only picture I had seen of him, the one on the jackets of his books, presented you with a dead-pan countenance. You half expected a number to be written across the bottom of the photo; it reminded you of the "Wanted For Robbery" pictures on the walls of American Post Offices. The reverse was true of the man in the flesh; he was all alive and aglow, like his books.

As a setting for my questions, I described Lewis' profound influence upon my Beloit colleague, Chad Walsh, whose excellent article on him had appeared in THE ATLANTIC MONTHLY. Lewis expressed his keen appreciation for Walsh's own volumes, *Stop Looking And Listen, An Invitation To The Christian Life,* and others. I then acknowledged my own indebtedness for innumerable Lewis ideas and pictures used in classroom and pulpit. Former students at Union College, Kentucky, had asserted: "C. S. Lewis is Soper's Bible." Amused, Lewis said, "You're welcome to any idea or picture you find useful." At once I thought of the fountain in *The Great Divorce* at which the pilgrim might drink, on his way to Deep Heaven, forthwith losing all sense of proprietorship over his own works, casting them like bread upon the waters of the world.

I mentioned the universal gratitude of Lewis' readers for his emphasis upon Christ as Son of God and Son of Man, and for his defense, like Chesterton's, of both Reason and Romanticism. It had sometimes been observed, however, that there was little emphasis in Lewis' books upon the Third Person in the Multiple Personality, God. Lewis reminded me of the short treatise accorded the Holy Spirit in *Beyond Personality*. I recalled the idea there expressed that the Holy Spirit was the Voice in the soul urging the Christian to pray. Mr. Lewis asserted that it seemed the way of the Holy Ghost to work silently, and anonymously, within the soul, calling attention only to Christ. There was great danger in the endeavor to force Him to speak by introspective listening; what often became articulate upon this inward command was not the Voice of the Spirit but the Voice of suppressed egoism or lust, an irruption from the subconscious. He quoted Bishop Hooker to the same effect. The Spirit called us constantly to obey the known will of God, to devote our energies to Christ's actual service, not to seek the esoteric and the occult, nor to pry irreverently into His own Personality. The Holy Ghost had given us some information about Himself, but only enough for obedience to Christ. His great work was not to focus our thought upon Himself but to cleanse our souls in the love of the Father and the Son, to lead us gently to true repentance and faith, to impart to our needy spirits New Life, the Christ-Life, not originally our own. The Holy Ghost was not a Super-Egoist, but the soul's Surgeon.

I confessed that I had then read all the Lewis books except *The Abolition of Man* and the new volume, *Miracles*. I assumed the latter was based in part, which Lewis acknowledged, on George Macdonald's characterization of a miracle as a normal act of Divine Creation reduced in time by, and for, human understanding. I expressed keen appreciation for Lewis' collection of Macdonald paragraphs. In daily devotions, I had found Macdonald a Protestant Thomas À. Kempis. Mr. Lewis reiterated his own joy in Macdonald, and explained, smiling, that the bearded gentleman in the painting above the fireplace was not Macdonald, as I had imagined, but his own ancestor, in no sense like the Nonconformist saint.

Exactly what kept us, I asked, from reunion with Rome? I quoted Christopher Dawson's urgent summons to all Christians to settle their secondary differences and unite, that a confused political and economic effort for World Fellowship might be given the spiritual vision to succeed. In point of history, Dawson had said, a universal Christian Church had created, and a divided Church had shattered, Western Unity. Only a re-united Church could reassemble the scattered fragments of Christian Civilization.

Lewis' thought about Rome was comprehensive yet simple. The difficulty with joining the Roman Church was that you were, so to speak, "buying a pig in a poke"; you could not possibly know at what hour something new would be added, as essential for salvation, to the worship of Christ as God and Saviour. Rome had an unfortunate tendency to pile Pelion upon Ossa, in every generation to require allegiance to a growing set of ideas not only not in the New Testament, but clearly foreign to its letter and alien to its spirit. Rome's addition of transubstantiation, the immaculate conception, papal infallibility, the worship of the Blessed Virgin, etc., I sugested, might possibly have arisen from dissatisfaction with mere faith in Christ, perhaps even from lack of faith in Christ. The Roman Church seemed to feel that something more glamorous than the Cross was needed to make Christianity convincing. Mr. Lewis agreed that "Christ alone" appeared insufficient to Roman Christians, but stressed the opposite failure as characteristically Protestant, the progressive discarding of Christianity's central ideas. If Romans seemed busily adding to the Gospel, he said, Protestants seemed as busily subtracting from it.

In Romanism, the doctrine of papal infallibility, of comparatively late origin, said Lewis, meant finally that the Pope could add any number of new requirements to the Gospel command of repentance and faith, and the Roman would be required to meet them all. Classical Christianity could have no sympathy with the process of addition, condemned by the Lord when He found it among the Pharisees — the superimposition upon the commandments of God of the traditions of men.

Mr. Lewis stated that he often felt more at home with Romans than with extreme Anglo-Catholics, who had passed, he said, into a worse state of ecclesiastical Rigor Mortis. He was not opposed to what was often called Rome's liturgical paganism. Color, in the service of the Gospel, and Tradition, the outcome of living faith, were wholly desirable.

If union were ever achieved between Protestantism and Romanism, should God please to bring it about, it would come, in all likelihood, not from the clergy but from the people, not from officialdom, uniformly slow to react to spiritual Light, but from godly charity, and a deepened common commitment to Christ as Lord, among all Christians. An ecclesiastical hierarchy, continued Lewis, was like a skeleton, important but the most mineral and dead part of the body. An archbishop, he said, was rather like a shoulder-blade. A skeleton reacted only after a considerable time lapse, and if the silent operation of the Holy Ghost produced unity, officials would wake up one day and find their constituencies united. The hierarchies would then come straggling after, like Mary's lamb, or make way for new leadership.

We did not discuss the point, but the essential problem of the United Nations, of world political fellowship, seems of like nature. As Toynbee has described it, Democracy and Industrialism, ecumenical in character, as new wine poured into the old bottles of deified parochial states, have produced the enormity of Nationalism; whole peoples have earnestly endeavored to exterminate one another. These parochial sovereignties, in Toynbee's view, had to make way for free world political fellowship, or destroy one another. Political hierarchies were the enemies of mankind insofar as they obstructed world democracy. They had to be shouldered aside or transcended, if man was not to perish from the Earth. Is not this the essential problem of world Christian fellowship — to transcend deified parochial denominations?

As preparation for Christian re-union, it seemed clearly necessary that Protestantism become genuinely Christian. Exactly how, I enquired, did Mr. Lewis believe Evangelical Protestantism might obtain a new lease on Life? What did I mean, Lewis asked, by the word "Evangelical"? I explained that the term had been adopted, quite tentatively, among many American leaders to distinguish a transforming faith in Christ as God and Saviour from Relativism on the one hand and Fundamentalism on the other. Mr. Lewis felt that a better term for the position described would be simply "Christianity," or "Classical Christianity," or "Incarnational Christianity." In England, he said, the adjective "Evangelical" meant salvation by faith without works, a subjective experience without objective obedience, a purely personal affair disdaining the holy fellowship, and necessary discipline, of Church and Society.

I acknowledged that the term "plain, central Christianity," as C. S. Lewis had used it in his Introduction to Athanasius' *The Incarnation Of The Word Of God,* seemed preferable, since the adjective "Evangelical" apparently had a double meaning.

"Plain, central Christianity," said Mr. Lewis, had not only not died in England, but, according to recent polls taken at random along city streets, it had proven the dominant Faith among Theists everywhere. A meager and inarticulate dissenting minority existed, but not in numerical strength. If American Protestantism had bogged down in the Deistic Slough-of-Despond, from which European Christianity had emerged in the latter half of the nineteenth century, the serious Christians who remained had simply "to believe, to preach, and to pray" in every conceivable way, in entire obedience to the Spirit and with full trust in God. The Light of the Gospel, uplifted among the people, would still dispel the darkness. Mr. Lewis has himself found many literary forms effective pulpits for the declaration of the Faith.

In modern life, two strong movements, he acknowledged, clearly existed side by side, one of disintegration, the other of recovery. It could be, if God so pleased, he said, that the resurrection of central Christianity, and perhaps a parliamentary reunion with Rome, would come about only through external pressure and persecution from an atomic and secular age. The early Church had been continually re-born in Power and Grace under Roman persecution; Protestantism had been similarly strengthened under Roman clerical attack. The League of Nations, born with Woodrow Wilson as obstetrician, had grown, despite considerable attack,

71

to become the United Nations. The Christian had to labor with a keen sense of urgency, yet he could not afford the luxury of discouragement; when he had lost his Hope, he had parted with his Faith and would soon part with his Love.

In the interview with Etienne Gilson, I had mentioned that no philosophy of politics appeared in C. S. Lewis' books. There was, I acknowledged, no reason to expect everything from one man. Gilson had described Lewis as "a pure theologian."

I therefore asked, "What of Christianity and politics?" C. S. Lewis immediately declared that in his estimation Christianity did not recommend specific planks for political platforms. For example, he said, when the Lord commanded that the five thousand be fed, He did not give a set of cooking recipes. Nonetheless, Lewis continued, it was not to be assumed that Christianity was neutral on political issues. It was a great nuisance really, for it demanded that political parties cease building their followings through misrepresentation. If any political program offered bread at the cost of spiritual freedom, Christianity was forced to say, "The hungry will have to remain hungry." Christianity approved of social planning provided individuals were not pushed around for their own good. The Christian pattern included individual moral responsibility and the protection of minorities. Christianity was neither neutral politically nor specific about procedure. It would see the hungry fed, but not at the cost of coercive collectivism, which recognized no moral law above its own will, which turned men into machines, into beings more terrible than beasts.

Insofar as postwar nations were like eight men in mid-Atlantic on a life raft, Collectivism was clearly a practical necessity. Marxian metaphysics were not involved. Community distribution of limited resources was obviously inescapable.

And what, I asked, were we going to do with Russia? "I should have thought," said Lewis promptly, "that you would have fought her." Russia, he said, had proven as alien to democratic diplomacy as Hitler's Germany ever was, as completely given to lying and stealing in the national self-interest, as tyrannical, despotic, and imperialistic. Where were we, he enquired, in our current relations with Russia if not at the precise dilemma of 1937 with its policy of appeasement? Christianity had never countenanced powerful and organized Evil. A Christian policy required firm resistance against the Russian infiltration of Europe; if war came, it would be Russia's decision. C. S. Lewis shared this attitude with Reinhold Niebuhr; the idea was scandalously clear and shockingly simple. Christianity had no part with either Marxism or Racism; it was rather the historic Champion of Ecumenical Spiritual Freedom.

Mr. Lewis did not feel qualified to speak on technical details in political economy. He urged that I interview the Papist, Barbara Ward, an expert economist. "Besides," he added, with a jolly smile, "she is the most beautiful woman in all England; she looks like you imagine Shakespeare's heroines ought to look." This C. S. Lewis had little in common with the austere recluse pictured in standard reports. I doubted his haste to lock himself in his rooms when a woman was known to be trespassing on the Magdalene Quadrangle. I thought at once of the chaste but earthy romanticism in the closing chapters of *That Hideous Strength*.

But how, I enquired at parting, had Lewis managed to get so much done? Had there been a hallowed daily period upon which intrusion had not been tolerated? Quite the contrary, he said. He had had to write by snatches, between walking the dog and peeling the potatoes. England had too few housekeepers, and his aged mother then required considerable care. There had been no mythological bachelor's retreat into an Ivory Tower, but the complex responsibilities of a willing, but occupied, domestic.

T. S. ELIOT

My first acquaintance with T. S. Eliot's work was the common one, which is also in a way the worst possible one — a study of his early poetry. It is the worst possible approach for two reasons: his early poems represent the cynical and transitional periods in his spiritual pilgrimage; though simple enough in central idea, they are the least clear and understandable part of his overall output. Had I begun with a later masterpiece like *Four Quartets*, in all probability his finest achievement, a better introduction would have been provided. At the time of my first approach to his writing I was a senior at DeLand, Florida's Stetson University; I was, as well, an unconditional disciple of John Dewey and a thoroughgoing atheist. Professor A. J. Gordis of Stetson's English department, now succeeded by my friend and former colleague, Byron H. Gibson, no doubt regarded me as his prize nuisance, and with ample justification. In any case, Mr. Gordis succeeded admirably in exciting my interest in Louis Untermeyer's *Contemporary British and American Poetry*. We spent long hours with *J. Alfred Prufrock*, T. S. Eliot's Caspar Milquetoast dilettante; we wandered through *The Waste Land* and x-rayed *Hollow Men*. In spite of my atheism I found myself in sympathy with Eliot's caustic criticism of American cultural and spiritual sterility. On the whole, however, I came away from this first contact with Eliot an interested and puzzled auditor, but in no sense a disciple.

Among the many treasures for which I am indebted to Lynn Harold Hough's Drew Seminar in *The Christian Criticism Of Life* was a deepened appreciation of T. S. Eliot as Christian Humanist and profound analyst of contemporary society. In numerous critical essays the man and his many-sided message were presented. The names, Irving Babbitt, Paul Elmer More, and T. S. Eliot became associated in my mind, and in the minds of my colleagues, as a humanist triumvirate: Babbitt the critical humanist, content to attack the humanitarian fallacy on behalf of stoic restraint; More and Eliot the critical humanists turned Christian. It was More whom I followed on his journey from the inner moral war of *The Shelburne Essays* to the classical Christianity of *The Greek Tradition* and the Synthesis of *The New Shelburne Essays*.

T. S. Eliot increasingly captured my affection on his own account, for he was in every way a fascinating personality, an atheist turned Anglican, an American turned Englishman — at once an editor, essayist, lecturer, poet, and banker.

My Castle Heights congregation in White Plains, New York, heard a great deal about T. S. Eliot, and not a few new members were required to read Eliot's *The Idea Of A Christian Society* as part of their preparation for adequate Churchmanship. It was in the study of this book, and in particular of its appendices, that

I myself was converted from doctrinaire Pacifism to Christian Responsibility.

Since that time I have made constant use of T. S. Eliot in sanctuary and classroom. During the past year seven Beloit upperclassmen have elected, in my department, to read all his published work, and to round off the research with an essay. These endeavors to isolate Eliot's central ideas have been, on more than one occasion, of genuine penetration.

To have visited London and not to have interviewed T. S. Eliot would have been a serious omission. It was sharply unfortunate that Mr. Eliot had been forced to undergo a serious operation at the London Clinic. Eleven days of convalescence had passed, however, and, informed that I had called to see him, he invited me cordially to his room. Under the circumstances he might well have been short of patience, yet I found him instead the incarnation of kindly grace, and not ungrateful for a word of honest tribute from an American admirer.

At his request, to identify my intellectual interests, I listed the subjects of my published essays: P. E. More, Kierkegaard, Augustine, Francis of Assisi, Dostoyevsky, and Sorokin. T. S. Eliot then treated at some length my question concerning the relationship between Christian Humanism, Existentialism, and Thomism. It was his opinion that a close connection did in fact exist between Existentialism and Christian Humanism in a common preoccupation with actual individuals, choosing painfully and joyfully their personal way in faith and life. This was not, of course, due to any historical continuity between the two systems. Christian Humanism and Thomism were also similar, since both were structural as well as personal, viewing life as Sub-Human, Human, and Divine. Here also, however, there was little external historical connection. The question was empirical, for individual Christian Humanists might be closer to Thomas or to Kierkegaard, depending on their interests. A Christian Humanist who emphasized the three levels, science, philosophy, and theology, would be closer to Thomas; one who stressed the soul's decisive pilgrimage would incline to Kierkegaard.

Christian Humanism, uniting the structuralism of Thomas and the existentialism, as well as the Socratic dialectic, of Kierkegaard, seemed the best possible Synthesis. On the common ground of Christian Humanism the Romans, Maritain, Gilson, and Dawson, and the Protestants, Berdiaeff, Niebuhr, and Eliot, were essentially of one Catholic mind.

I enquired whether Protestantism and Romanism might not find creative fellowship on the common basis of Christian Humanism. Eliot suggested two obstacles to union: the shattered theology of Protestantism, and the intransigence of the papacy. Classical Christians, whether in Roman or Protestant Communions, were already aware of basic identity; from spiritual community objective union might indeed grow. Rome's historic tendency, the tendency of any totalitarian system, to burn at the stake dissenting minorities, was the great Roman obstacle to Union. The Protestant difficulty was a fissiparous tendency, common to democratic organizations, a trend toward theological anarchy, ethical solipsism, and denominational diversity. The Protestant disintegration, in part, was now countered by the World Council of Churches, and perhaps even more effectively, by a considerable revival of articulate Theology. Mr. Eliot mentioned the Congregationalist, C. H. Dodd of Cambridge, eminent New Testament interpreter, as a noteworthy example of the return of prodigal Protestantism to classical Christianity.

We discussed Paul Elmer More at some length. T. S. Eliot mentioned his life-long acquaintance with the great American Anglican, a friendship which had begun years ago in St. Louis. Our conversation thus led directly to American Protestantism, with its seeming confusion of tongues. I was heartened to hear T. S. Eliot's opinion that English Christianity had largely recovered whatever ground it had lost to the arid rationalism of the eighteenth and nineteenth centuries. A dissenting minority, without articulate leadership, said Eliot, was patiently tolerated. Nineteenth century unbelief, now feeble in Europe, was, he said, still strong in the United States. The obvious American need, therefore, was the renewed teaching of the Christian Ideas in universities and colleges, at present more or less theologically illiterate. Basic Christianity had to be given in larger quantity and in improved quality to the members of Churches, to parents, to young people, and to the children in the home. Nothing could be achieved until Christian Theology replaced the religious vacuum sometimes characteristic of the American mind. It was not so much that Americans had rejected classical Christianity, and had turned deliberately to stoicism at best or epicureanism at worst. Actually, Americans had seldom been granted an acquaintance with the Subject. The distortions of Fundamentalism, or the "subtractions" of Relativism, had focused American attention. Intelligent men, faced exclusively with these false alternatives, had chosen the "subtractions" of Relativism. Religious enthusiasts, confronted with the same alternatives, had chosen the Fundamentalist intellectual Nihilism. In the excitement, classical Christianity had been lost to view. American Christianity was doing remarkably well, under the circumstances. It was beyond doubt a clear example of the miraculous labor of the Holy Spirit that American Christianity had so well survived its equally-virulent Fundamentalist and Relativist epidemics.

America desperately needed, he said, a great revival of classical Christian Theology. In particular the American university mind had become theologically uneducated. Confused adolescent mentalities could not be made coherent without a basic theological renaissance. American colleges for some time had been engaged, it appeared, in the manufacture of religious illiterates. Youth had been graduate essentially, that is, *humanly,* uneducated. The teaching of Christian Theology, once a responsibility of public education, had been left to the Home and the Church. But the parents, to whom the religious nurture of the young had thus been entrusted, were themselves second or third generation illiterates with nothing significant to teach. Until parents relearned the meaning and history of Christianity, exactly how could they impart a religious nurture worth mentioning to the little people? The Churches, often led by Fundamentalist or Relativist ministers, gifted neither with words nor ideas, frequently did their best to obscure the Christian Faith. Appointed teachers in Church Schools, who labored heroically in the dismal lack of information, were more or less, he said, "the blind leading the blind."

An unfortunate result of the American habit of teaching Christianity, in sentimental form, and only to children, had been the widespread assumption that Christianity was intellectually childish. When young people reached the age of sixteen, they concluded that religion was beneath their serious attention. Young people needed the realization that Christianity was primarily an adult affair, mature rather than childish; thus it would be possible to excite their curiosity and arouse their admiration. Mr. Eliot approved, at the college level, semester reading projects and research essays in Christian primary sources. He was convinced that the study of Christianity's major personalities, past and present, in Universities and in Churches, would restore to modern youth a natural respect for Christian thought.

A minority revival of Christian education, Mr. Eliot believed, did in fact exist in the United States. One could teach and pray, in the confident hope that the Candle, brought from under the bushel and placed upon the candlestick, would give Light to all.

T. S. Eliot's essays on the meaning of Western post-war culture, he acknowledged, were shortly to be published.

I enquired whether T. S. Eliot considered C. S. Lewis a legitimate Christian Romanticist. Had there been time I would have cited Lewis' reference in *Pilgrim's Regress* to T. S. Eliot as one of "The Pale Men," living a cloistered "life of the mind" withdrawn from the common humanity. C. S. Lewis' book had been sub-titled, *In Defense Of Christianity, Reason, and Romanticism,* and all his books, as his readers know, are remarkable flights of the imagination though securely based upon classical Christianity. I am not at all sure that C. S. Lewis would still regard T. S. Eliot as emotionally anemic. Quite probably the reference was to Eliot's early negativism. I was interested in evoking, if possible, any reverse estimate Eliot might have in mind. C. S. Lewis, asserted T. S. Eliot, had been deeply influenced by Charles Williams, certainly a legitimate Christian Romanticist. There had always been room within Christian fellowship for men of diverse temperaments. I was myself impressed, from my interviews with the two men, with the Christian

Classicism of Eliot, and the Christian Romanticism of Lewis. Both leaders clearly shared one sovereign commitment to Christ the Lord of Life.

T. S. Eliot expressed his conviction that the political terms "right-wing" and "left-wing" no longer had any clear meaning, particularly in England. A tremendous transition was in full progress on all sides. There were perhaps two systems with which Christianity would be forever at war — bureaucratic collectivism, denying the individual, on the one hand, and democratic anarchy, denying the group, on the other. A balance between the necessities of the community and the freedom of the individual seemed the difficult achievement, but, as Eliot has written in *The Idea Of A Christian Society,* "here as hereafter, the alternative to Hell is Purgatory."

ARNOLD J. TOYNBEE

There are scholars great and small, but there is only one Toynbee, standing to all others, it seems, as the complete to the partial. I first heard his name in Lynn Harold Hough's Graduate Seminar at Drew University, where several essays, based chiefly upon the hurried scanning of the first three of Toynbee's many-volumed *The Study Of History,* and therefore failing to perceive the Christian vigor of volumes four to six, and the telefinalist prophecy of the later products, their word of profound Hope, were presented cautiously by Ph.D. candidates awaiting critical attack. For one reason or another these introductions were then insufficient to arouse my interest. Perhaps it was entirely my own fault, but it may also have been because the multiplexity of Toynbee's arguments and the prodigality of his illustrations, as screened through the minds of particular essayists, did not reveal the very great clarity, the exalted simplicity, of his basic conclusions.

Again and again, however, I heard his name, and always in connection with some remarkable insight, until at length, after giving six months to Dostoyevsky and a year to Sorokin, I resolved to devote as much time as might be necessary to the London University historian, Director of the Royal Institute of International Affairs. I was particularly eager to complete the patient perusal of the then six volume *Study Of History* before interviewing the man himself. A Beloit student suggested recently that Toynbee quotations then appeared in my classroom lectures around the beginning of the second semester, hence the rough estimate that four months were consumed in the reading. Because I could read him only in the evenings, and occasionally on trains and in hotel rooms between addresses, the time required was greater than it should have been. I might have finished the six volumes more quickly but for the sheer pleasure of reading the copious footnotes, in which so often pearls beyond price were embedded.

The fact that I have formed a keen affection for Toynbee will probably be evident enough, without the confession. Evening after evening Mrs. Soper, reading Huxley or Lewis or Sayers at her side of the room, heard me emerge from a passage with a sigh of sheer delight and exclaim, "God bless Toynbee!" Having completed the six volumes I considered that I was then approximately half way through Toynbee's works in print. I later enjoyed the earlier volumes on international affairs, before rounding off the sequence with the latest volumes and the writing of an essay for *Religion In Life*.

Mrs. Toynbee, the Veronica M. Boulter to whom as his efficient secretary Mr. Toynbee has acknowledged a profound indebtedness, was kind enough to arrange with her husband the hour for our interview, and to phone this information to my hotel. When I returned to my rooms, after an exhilarating evening punting on the Thames with my friends, the Raymond Stanleys in Surbiton, the phone message, a happy word indeed, awaited me. In the morning, while anticipating the interview, I talked briefly on the phone with Dorothy L. Sayers, out of reach in Essex. Her voice was quite as charming as her books, half mystery novels, half theological treatises, are amazing. My essay on her work later appeared in *Religion In Life*.

When the hour finally arrived, I was led through a labyrinth of halls, elevators, and passage ways into the private Sanctum at Chatham House where the Toynbees work together across double desks. Mr. Toynbee himself arose to greet me, and saw to it that I was seated comfortably. Both Toynbees laughed aloud at the following anecdote. When I read my essay on Sorokin at the Southern Society for the Philosophy of Religion, Asheville, North Carolina, during the discussion which followed, I quoted liberally from Toynbee, and discovered another professor, Meyers of Roanoke College, Virginia, who had read him. Later I asked Mr. Meyers, "Do you think God knows anything Toynbee does not know?" At once he replied, "God may know a few things about the future that Toynbee does not know, very little about the past."

I expressed my personal indebtedness to Arnold J. Toynbee for the tremendous pleasure and profit his volumes had afforded me, mentioning that I had found them also of great devotional value, had indeed quoted from them, in pulpit as well as in classroom, times without number. Mr. Toynbee was kind enough to regard this as a tribute, and his eyes were warm with friendly gratitude. Throughout the interview I was impressed that I had found the kindliest man, and the noblest Christian, I had ever met. I felt that he might well have written the First Epistle of St. John. He seemed eager to know my opinion on each of the issues we discussed, and this intellectual magnanimity, I am convinced, was not a drawing room policy but rather the evidence of a natural humility and a sensitive curiosity.

I asked how he had completed so much work in one lifetime. He explained that he withdrew to Yorkshire when a bout of writing was required, giving his mornings and, reluctantly, the time from tea to supper, to the work.

Early in our interview I raised the problem of Pacifism. In France Toynbee had been cited in my hearing as a Pacifist, and I had resolved to find if this were true, because, in spite of the colossal attention in his work to the things that make for peace and his recurrent analysis of the tragedy of civil warfare between Western nations, I had not believed him guilty of the Biblical Literalism, nor of the false sentimentality, sometimes characteristic of practical rather than ideal Pacifism. His prophetic emphasis upon the necessity of a cessation of fratricidal strife within Christendom should perhaps be presented more fully at this point. Throughout his volumes all history marches in solemn procession to declare in chorus that every extinct or dying Civilization went into decline precisely at the moment when the disease of militarism produced fratricidal internecine warfare between its deified parochial sovereign States. In our time the cry of havoc and the unleashing of the dogs of war have been greatly intensified in destructiveness, not so much because of atomic energy and its vastly enlarged bombs, but, in Toynbee's view, mainly because the twin ecumenical drives of Industrialism and Democracy, poured like new wine into the old bottles of nationalistic States, have produced the enormity of total war, in which whole peoples, and for exalted reasons, have sought to exterminate one another.

It is the contention of Toynbee's volumes that a worldwide economy, required by modern machines and modern men, will break down inevitably unless one political world, uniting freedom with fellowship, can be established as its necessary framework. Uniformly throughout history the breakdown of political union among the States which have formed a Civilization, a breakdown issuing directly from prior spiritual schism, has resulted in internecine warfare until all competing States have been equally destroyed, through mutually administered knock-out blows, or until one power has emerged, through the elimination of its competitors, to establish a despotic Universal State, the last stage before tragic disintegration — as in the story of the Roman Empire — the period of breakdown however serving in fact as chrysalis of the growing Christian Civilization.

This is, in brief, Toynbee's published account of the breakdowns of all the extinct or expiring Civilizations of our Earth. Only one Civilization, in his view, continues to be a "going concern" — Western or Christian Civilization, and we seem to have reached mid-way in the familiar antepenultimate stage before complete decline— the stage of civil warfare between the nationalistic States into which our Western Christian Society has become articulated. Yet no external necessity compels us to go the way of all flesh. The outcome is not determined, either by our stars or by our hormones. The decision lies with us. If we will not make world democracy a living reality, a period may be written in blood at the end of our sentence.

One readily comprehends, therefore, how weighty a demand for Peace emerges from Toynbee's *Study Of History,* and it is understandable that he has been interpreted as a Pacifist. Indeed, his insistence that throughout history the pirate or aggressive nations, prepared for war, have always lost, and the more moral, the more civilized and restrained, like Athens over Sparta, have uniformly won, seems a direct summons to absolute Pacifism.

It was the more of interest, therefore, to have it directly from Toynbee's lips that he was not, and has never been, a Pacifist. He has been actively engaged, in any labor for which his specialized capacities have best fitted him, in support of Britain's efforts in both World Wars. He could understand that individuals, revolted by the horrors of war, might at times become absolute Pacifists, being Literalists in interpreting parts of the Bible, or seeking to live in isolation on some imagined margin of the page of life. However, he did not himself share the Pacifist position, believing that real resistance had to be offered mankind's organized enemies — if only that free men might have the opportunity to work out their own political salvation in fear and trembling. I quoted L. P. Jacks' statement to me that it had been wrong to wage war against Hitler, but not to have done so would have been a greater wrong. Mr. Toynbee regarded this an admirable summary of the essential truth. Any organized effort to coerce free men into goose-stepping collectivism, he said, whether out of Germany or out of Russia, could only be stopped by a greater effort in the service of moral ideas and in defense of human freedom.

A major implication, in all of Toynbee's books, is the urgent necessity of "one spiritual world" to provide the unity of soul essential to political and economic peace. This idea emerges with crystal clarity in a retrospective analysis of Western History, as both Toynbee and Christopher Dawson have shown. It was not political or economic unity which gave birth to a universal Christian ideology, but the exact reverse. Christianity "found Western man a barbarian," a raw savage, "and has promoted him to his present Lordship of creation." In Christianity's Universal Church the glories of an extinct Hellenic Civilization, to which Western Civilization is affiliated, were gathered up. From the matrix of that Universal Church the West was born. It is the common warning of Toynbee and Dawson that the certain way to oblivion is paved with unrealized good intentions; that for the children of Western Civilization to "forsake the God Who made them and lightly to esteem the Rock of their salvation" is the broad avenue leading to destruction.

Thus a clear modern necessity is "one spiritual world," in fact whether or not in name. With this in mind I enquired whether, in Toynbee's estimation, there was hope either of objective or of subjective reunion with Rome. He mentioned at once the demonstrated intransigence of the papacy, Rome's crystallized conception of its self-sufficiency, its historic unwillingness to regard Protestantism as an Ally, its refusal to acknowledge any legitimate labor of the Holy Spirit outside the Roman Communion, its belief that it possesses by Divine Right an absolute monopoly on salvation — yet its equal insistence, with Pius XII, that men of conscience in any land or language or religion can be, and are, members of the Soul, if not of the Body, of Christ. He considered a more important, and more available, immediate objective Christian reunion within Protestantism, and approved the good work of the World Council of Churches, uniting denominations in a wholesome fellowship around the common Kingship of Christ.

Clearly the World Council had taken the necessary first step toward reunion in Christendom, Mr. Toynbee believed — the reassertion of the essentials of the Faith, as distinct from its non-essential particular elements developed in time and space. A common awareness of central Christianity, newly awakened throughout all Christian Communions, said Toynbee, was, and would continue to be, the strongest force, alike of mind and spirit, for the eventual lessening of Roman and Protestant sectarianism. Essential Christianity embraced many Classical Christian Ideas, but perhaps most definitively, in Toynbee's opinion, was focused in the recognition of Christ "not as a Deputy of God but as Himself God." Mr. Toynbee agreed with C. S. Lewis that, in all likelihood, the Roman and Protestant hierarchies would follow, and not lead, in a common fellowship around essential Christianity. He disagreed with Maritain's statement that the false concept of the Divine Right of Kings had caused the Protestant Secession from Rome. In Toynbee's estimation, the deification of sovereign parochial States had been the result rather than the cause of that Secession. He did not share Gilson's view that the parliamentary principle, if accepted by the fifteenth century Popes when offered them in the form of the Conciliar Movement, would have destroyed the continuity and character of Romanism. It would rather have made possible the preservation of a desperately needed Western spiritual unity. He was not of one mind with Dawson's idea that irrational and revolutionary forces had been the determining causes in the Protestant cleavage of Christendom; they had rather been contributing factors.

We came thus to a consideration of major steps which had to be taken to recover essential Christianity within the whole of Christendom — in particular, since that seems to be our own direct responsibility, within Protestantism. Precisely what techniques of Evangelism, or what theological renaissance, I asked, would have to precede the Great Renewal? Toynbee was close to Kierkegaard in his answer. The obvious point of beginning was the same now as it had been in the earliest Christian centuries — not theoretical objectivity but subjective obedience among individual Christians. Christians in deed and word had always been the bridgeheads of Christian advance. If the people of the Churches could somehow manage to be also the people of Christ, the pagan or neo-pagan worldlings could not but be charmed into the Faith. Victorious Evangelism had always been existential rather than theoretical, involving Christians in person rather than Christians in print. As Woodrow Wilson had said, "You can refute arguments but not saints."

This individualization of Christianity did not by-pass the necessity of "a live theology"; it actually embraced it, for historic Christians, witnessing to the common Kingship of Christ by their deeds, had not acted without thought, but rather upon thought, had not lived their heroic lives around the absence but around the presence of central Christian beliefs.

"Being a Christian" was not primarily muscular activism, usually a substitute for the real thing. The root of the matter was always an interior affair of the obedient will, the dethronement of the Ego and the enthronement of the Lord, a sensitive responsiveness to the leading of His Spirit. Christian persons, set down anywhere in the world, tended to turn any hopeless Inferno into a hopeful Purgatorio.

Individual Christians were therefore Christianity's most effective "techniques". They were the real bridges from Christ to the pagan masses; nothing whatever could take their place. And, precisely because such personalities were Christ's witnesses among the people, they were also discoverers of subsidiary measures of practical procedure by which to offer Mankind the Avenue to Life. "Bridge-building" of every conceivable kind was the present Christian necessity, if ever Church-going were to become again a majority enterprise and an effective Christian education. Mrs. Toynbee, daughter of a minister of the Church of England, was urged by her husband to express her opinion on this point. It might indeed be, she said, that the average non-Church-goer in England and the United States tended to think like a Christian, in some degree. It was obvious, however, that no Christian advance could be made by persons who were always retreating from Christianity. Clearly the non-Church-goer would not long think, even superficially, like a Christian, unless a vigorous renewal occurred at the Source of his second-hand ideology.

The problem was two-fold. There was no point in building a bridge to the people, asserted Toynbee, unless the bridge led to Christianity. Often a bridge was constructed, but upon examination some ersatz religiosity had been substituted for Christianity at the near end. The people crossed but did not find the regenerating elixir of Faith. The opposite hazard was lethargy, the stalemate of keeping a true Christianity, like the candle described by the Lord, under a bushel. It was the City set upon a hill that could not be hid. The Light had to shine "among men", that they might see its good works, and glorify the Father in Heaven. There was possibly no way to ascertain which of these opposed miscarriages was the characteristic one in our time. Evangels of one sort or another seemed active on the one hand, but it did not always appear to be Christianity to which they were summoning the people. On the other hand, Christians were busily hiding their treasure in a field, apparently afflicted with an inferiority-complex. Clearly a Church with an inferiority mentality was as far from the True Faith as the fleet-footed messengers without the Message. Either failure was a luxury contemporary Christianity could ill afford.

Our discussion led at last to the Christian and his politics. The defining principle, said Toynbee, by which all political systems were to be judged, was the spiritual dignity of individual personality. All collectivisms, based upon a cancellation of individual responsibility, were alien to Christianity. This was clear enough after two General Wars, fought to preserve human rights and duties against coercive totalitarian encroachment. Perhaps less clear was the fact that Liberalism, which agreed that the individual personality must not be treated as a means, had largely departed from the Faith in which respect for individual worth had been born and without which it could not survive. Liberalism had cut the flower from its root, and, while admiring it, failed to see that it was dying. Group measures might well be taken to eliminate group distresses, but the individual, though a minority of one, had to be saved from the crushing majority. Group action, though issuing freely from the consent of the community, and not at all the product of collectivism and dictatorship, had to make room for the disagreeing minority (the Democratic Party in the White House for Republicans, or the Republican Party in the White House for Democrats), or itself become the enemy of spiritual, moral, and political freedom. Christianity demanded, here as elsewhere, a paradox; group action for the solution of group problems, and at the same time the defense of individual freedom against group aggression. At the one side were the hazards of anarchy, and at the other the even greater hazards of a crushing collectivism. Christianity sought the middle way, a difficult balance between the needs of the community and the freedom of individuals.

Man's social life, Toynbee asserted, could not be considered merely external, for the society of which man was a part included God, as well as human personalities, and therefore included an unbending Righteous Judgment, and a universal Redemptive Will, set above all action, both social and personal.

WILLIAM R. INGE

The gracious lady, Mrs. Inge, was kind enough to invite me to tea, and, while awaiting the appointed hour, I roamed about through the Churchyard and within the Sanctuary at Brightwell Berks. Parts of the building, the south arch, dated from the twelfth century, and both Roman and Anglican priests had ministered at its ancient altar. A few days earlier I had listened to the chants in St. Paul's Cathedral, where for twenty-three years William R. Inge had been the celebrated Dean. I had mused on the idea that the London Cathedral named for the first Non-Roman Apostle had been guided by Anglicanism's great Evangelical.

The Dean, then 87, possessed all the intellectual keenness of earlier years, and produced one epigram after another as we talked. I sat close to him, to assist in overcoming his slight handicap of deafness, and, with Mrs. Inge as original conversationalist and counselor, the interview, begun before tea, was continued afterward. I felt myself at times transported to another world, a world removed from two great wars, a society of Lords and Ladies, a spacious, gracious time. It was the Dean who brought me again and again, with his words of concern and wisdom, to the crises of the present.

My first enquiry concerned the Dean's estimate of current trends in Anglican theology. It was his reasoned conviction that contemporary Anglicanism suffered from a lack of original Christian thinkers. I pointed to the profound contributions of Paul Elmer More, T. S. Eliot, and Arnold J. Toynbee of the present, but he was thinking of previous generations and of professional theologians. He was sympathetic to the work of More and Eliot, and then sad that Toynbee's remaining volumes might not be completed in time for him to read them. He had recently reviewed the single volume summary of six Toynbee volumes, among his many articles for English journals, and was immensely pleased with the book. It was his critical opinion, however, that some of Toynbee's terms were misleading, in particular the term "Internal Proletariat." Christianity had never been, in his estimation, the religion of the Proletariat, as we understood the word today. In view of Marxian associations, a more exact and edifying term should have been substituted.

The Dean deplored the present surrender of L. P. Jacks to French New Testament criticism, which left nothing standing, and reduced Christ to an insignificant Galilean enthusiast. "A mountain might bring forth a mouse," said the Dean, smiling, "but a mouse could hardly bring forth a mountain." The Relativist denial of the Deity of Christ would add nothing to the stature of men, was at best the preaching of a negation. At the other extreme were the Anglo-Catholics, with whom the Dean had very little patience, for they were quite determined to do nothing to prevent a speedy surrender of liberty. There might be anarchy and solipsism in non-Roman Christianity, accompanying its accent on freedom, but there was "no point in putting on hand-cuffs to keep one's hands from shaking." Protestant mystics would never admit that their relation with God was less objective than that of the Church of the Middle Ages. The mystics believed in the objective reality of the God with Whom they communed, and were therefore guilty neither of anarchy nor solipsism, being obedient to one Will. Psychological talk about states of consciousness, and so forth, did not describe true prayer. Mystics were not worshipping states of consciousness, but God, and communing with His Spirit. To place Christianity again under despotic control would put Christianity in chains. It was not a chained and manacled Christianity that would save the world, but a Christianity free to use its full powers for the resurrection of the human spirit and the creation of a Free World.

Mrs. Inge considered the Christian teaching of the children a first step in modern spiritual recovery. To this end, parents had to be given thorough training in the great things of the Faith. Children could grow up only as pagans when their parents were religious illiterates. The wise parent who knew the Bible could make its stories live for young minds. She described the first time she had related the story of the Crucifixion to her youngest son, Richard, later killed in World War II just as he had become an ordained priest of the Church of England with a brilliant career before him. At the time of the story Richard had been considerably less than ten years of age. After Mrs. Inge had described in detail the Sacrifice of the Lamb of God, Richard had run out of the room in tears, and flung himself on the grass with arms outspread. "To think," he had sobbed, "that Jesus would do that for me. It hurts just to stretch out my arms." Until mothers, and fathers too, took it upon themselves to learn, and to teach, the New Testament stories meaningfully, how could the little ones "love God with all their hearts and love their neighbors as themselves?" It was the young imagination that had to be captured for Christ.

If Christians would not seek to nurture young minds in the love of Christ, they should remember that Communists and Nazis, presenting their conformist creeds to the young, were not so timid. The little minds were eager, and empty, and if they did not receive a Christian filling, they would receive a lesser one.

Dean Inge asserted that nowhere in the New Testament, and certainly not in the Old, was there any basis for the modern idea that all men were to be saved. If one started out with a false objective, would he not be quickly disillusioned? Christ said nothing about receiving everyone; the statement, "him that cometh I will not cast out," required men to come; only the few would inherit His Kind of Life. "Many are called, but few are chosen." The multitude, as Christ said, would be drawn to Him, if He were uplifted, but perhaps as admirers, not as disciples. Christ would never cast out those who came, and whosoever would might come, but the masses preferred the broad to the narrow way and could not be persuaded. Disciples were to be made, among all nations, but they were never expected to be majorities. They were rather to be the healing and redeeming minorities, the saving remnants, Christ's lights in dark societies. With this in mind, perhaps the work of Christ was going forward somewhat normally — not converting all men, to be sure, but converting as many as desired a Strength greater than their own, as many as were thus ordained to eternal Life.

The so-called "gloomy Dean" did not at any time, or in any degree, seem gloomy to me. Exactly the reverse mood seemed to be in all his thinking. A smile was perpetually hovering around the corners of his mouth, and in each dark problem of our generation he pointed out rather the hope than the despair. If he has been called "gloomy", it could only be because, like Jeremiah, he has lived in a time of disintegration whose follies were clear to him; yet, again like Jeremiah, when other voices offer counsels of despair, his voice speaks of light beyond tragedy.

He regarded himself as left-wing in theology and right-wing in politics, though upon definition his left-wing theology turned out to be Evangelical as opposed to Anglo-Catholic Anglicanism. He was neither a Fundamentalist nor a Unitarian, but a classical Christian, moved rather to Apostolic Zeal than to a weak lusting after the comfort of an authoritarian church. In description of his right-wing politics, he quoted a conversation with Winston Churchill, who had said to him: "Dean, I know what you are politically." "Yes," replied the Dean, "the last Whig." His interests lay, not with democracy, which he characterized as "rule by mass bribery", but with a leadership of merit, a responsible economy which sought to "render to every man his due." Socialism was simply a decadent democracy increasing the bribe offered to the masses in exchange for their freedom.

He seemed to have much in common with Churchill, whose address at Blenheim Palace I had been privileged to hear, and with

Robert Boothby, radical Tory M.P. from Aberdeen, whose striking lecture on British economy was delivered in my hearing at Oxford University. The essential Churchill emphasis was the doctrinaire quality of British Socialism, seeking with fanatical zeal to force its monistic dogma down the public throat, regardless of the evident consequences in decreased production, reduced exports, increased imports, enlarged public payrolls, and general mismanagement. Socialism was afflicted with schizophrenia: on the one hand it shouted the slogan, "We Work Or Want", and on the other pledged shorter hours and higher wages, paying no one for actual production, encouraging men to seek more money for less labor, and offering no liberation from a Tax Law which confiscated working men's wages beyond the barest minimum. In a time of labor shortage, the Socialist regime had added 450,000 functionaries to the national pay-roll whose only service to the nation had been to enlarge its bureaucracy, add to its already oppressive cost of government, and decrease its efficiency. These additional government employees, as Churchill put it, were "a positive obstacle to recovery." Socialism had thrown away profitable India and was then clinging desperately and at tremendous cost to profitless Palestine, had borrowed American money to rehabilitate British Industry and used it to purchase indulgences — fruit, candy, films, and tobacco. Any housekeeper knew that thrift, contrivance, and work would solve problems, but Socialism believed only that it did not matter how bad things became, as long as the misery was shared equally by everyone. (As a matter of fact, everyone in England, it seemed, spoke appreciatively of Socialist Distribution, and, at the same time, deplored the Socialist inability to achieve Production.) The strong were forced to slacken their production pace to that of the slothful and the weak. The Nationalized Mines, with more machinery and at higher cost, had produced less coal than before Nationalization — 15,000,000 tons a year less than in 1940. Private ownership had proven its greater flexibility. The miners had already discovered that they could strike more easily against the Government than against private capital. Recovery could only come about under a leadership not committed to some economic dogma, some monistic formula requiring a sheer despotism to make it work, but to an intelligent grappling with problems as they arose. The strong should be allowed, and indeed encouraged, to produce as rapidly and with as few hindrances as possible for the well-being of all.

The Dean, unlike Churchill, believed, he said, that England's War with Hitler, which had cost her sons, her liberty, and her money, had been a luxury she could not afford. England similarly could afford no war with Russia, whatever the United States might decide to do. There was much to be said for the Quakers and their Pacifism, he added, as well as for their mysticism — their personal, living relationship with the Divine Spirit.

We discussed briefly the basic cultural differences between England and America. England could not sell her art treasures, her museums, for American imports, as I suggested in jest: America would have to produce her own masterpieces by the patient processes of genius and wisdom; she could not revel in a culture not her own. American culture, Mrs. Inge believed, insofar as it was characterized by machinery, speed, intellectual thinness, and religious illiteracy, had its tasks ahead. It was difficult for her to imagine young Americans being nurtured without the love of Holy Communion, with meager intellectual and spiritual cultivation. Perhaps conditions in America were much better than reports indicated. America, a young nation, she said, had undoubtedly a great future.

I suggested that Lord Macaulay may have been right when he predicted that America would be destroyed by internal barbarians in the middle of the Twentieth Century. Mrs. Inge felt that destruction by internal barbarians was a possibility not merely in America, but also on the Continent and in England.

At length the hour of departure drew near. I was privileged to sign my name in the great Book of Guests, and to pledge, at Mrs. Inge's invitation, to present to her my wife and daughters, whose pictures she had seen, on an early visit to England. It was the Dean who walked with me past the little lake with its colossal Weeping Elm to the gate, close by the Church and the monument to Brightwell's war dead. As I left with his blessing, I knew that I had visited a saint with mature benevolence and penetration.

THE FRENCH EXISTENTIALIST POINT OF VIEW

Arrived in Paris, I started my search for the mysterious Sartre, or, should he prove unavailable, for his fellow Existentialist, Albert Camus. Neither name was listed in the Paris phone book; I realized that obstacles, perhaps insurmountable, might block my way. At the Post Office, Vaugirard and Tournon, across from the Senat, a tall, blackhaired French youth came to my aid. He had spent boyhood years in England, he explained, and was now employed at a Paris book store. He bade me accompany him to his "Librarie" where he believed he would find the desired information. He fingered energetically but in vain through several reference catalogues. However, the address of a publisher who had issued Existentialist literature was forthcoming; I left the courteous French youth with many words of gratitude. In half an hour I entered the hallway of No. 5, rue Sebastien-Bottin, and, within a few minutes, was received by M. Raymond Queneau, literary advisor of the publishing firm of Gallimard, and, as well, of LES TEMPS MODERNES, the Existentialists' French review. Had I come to Paris a week earlier, said Queneau, both Sartre and Camus would have welcomed my questions. Unfortunately, Sartre had but just left for Algiers, and Camus for Avignon. Clearly, time would not allow me to follow either writer, but M. Queneau, through long association with both men, and participation as critic in their publications, was amply prepared as their spokesman and interpreter. Frankly and courteously Queneau answered all my queries as, he believed, Sartre and Camus would have answered them.

Let me, at this point, briefly summarize three root ideas in Sartre's Existentialism, lest questions and answers be misunderstood. The first Existentialist idea is simple enough: *Existence precedes essence* — that is, man is the sole creator of his own values, his standards, his principles, his morality. Truth does not precede human personality, but follows it, is indeed created by it. In familiar words, there is no God except Man, no Source above man for the ideas he discovers and the values he adopts — the position as well of Sir Julian Huxley. The second root idea in the Existentialism of Sartre and Camus is also clear; man is not happy that there is no God; on the contrary, he thinks it an horrible thing that there should be no God. Man is painfully aware that he is a free, spiritual being who must create his principles and choose his way. He is therefore a creature of anguish, of forlornness, of despair, precisely because he is a creature also of responsibility. He stands or falls by the virtue or vice of the values he invents, by the choices he makes. There is no God, no Guide, no Friend, no Helper in the universe. Man is horribly alone; he is not even to be identified with nature, for nature is ruled by necessity. Man can say, "No!"; he is therefore ruled not by biology, but by the principles he has created, by the uncoerced choices he has made. He is a moral or spiritual creature who can trace his freedom neither to God nor to biology. He knows nothing of his origin. He simply exists, and only with his existence as a free being can thought begin. The third basic Existentialist idea is Involvement. A man must risk something; he must become entangled in the experience of his fellow men to assist them in the pursuit of freedom. A man cannot remain aloof from risk, from human involvement; at any cost in suffering and sacrifice, he must become immersed in the human struggle, never justifying himself, accepting the common forlornness and anguish, to attain the freedom which is man's highest good.

From these three roots French Existentialism has grown; by this time you may have anticipated my questions. I explained my first query thus: "In view of Sartre's emphasis upon the freedom or spirituality of the human personality, is it enough to leave unanswered the question of the origin of this non-material life? Sartre frequently uses the expression, 'Man *is thrust* into the anguish of freedom,' as though man had been thrust *by someone* or something. Existentialism then refuses to consider further the question of origin. This is a metaphysical tour de force; the question cannot be left unanswered by the soul." M. Queneau acknowledged that Sartre had put forth no answers to this question. He had denied, however, any natural or biological origin for the spiritual freedom with which man is cursed or blessed. On the other hand, in Sartre's denial of God he had similarly disposed of any spiritual Source for man's spirituality. He had simply dropped the subject, and had proceeded to construct his philosophy upon the present fact of man's painful freedom. I asked, "If there is no God, and if nature has not produced man's freedom, what can be said but that man's freedom has produced itself, that man is, perhaps through evolution, his own creator?" M. Queneau stated that nothing further on this topic had been expressed by either Sartre or Camus.

It is clear that this question cannot be answered, it can only be by-passed, by Sartre's Existentialism. What man does with the fact of his freedom is of undisputed importance. Here Sartre and Marcel have ground in common. Both Christians and non-Christians are confronted with the anguish, and glory, of freedom. Yet the question of the origin of freedom seeks an answer, for the answer itself may determine the nature and use of freedom. Even from a purely utilitarian or pragmatic point of view, this prior metaphysical question cannot be wholly ignored.

Christianity comes to this question with an answer partly from reason and partly from reason self-transcended, that is, from Revelation. The argument from reason is that freedom could not have been created by necessity, hence nature might be the mother but not the Father of man's spirituality. Likewise, reason itself demands that from nothing nothing comes; hence man who finds himself free could not have created his own freedom; he cannot be his own creator. Only one possibility remains, on rational grounds, namely, that a Power and an Intelligence capable of producing man's freedom must have created man. Revelation moves on beyond these arguments from reason to declare that God is, that He is the Rewarder of them that diligently seek Him, that it is He that hath made us and not we ourselves, that He has moved of His own redemptive volition out of pure spirit into history — supremely in the Person, Jesus Christ. The answer of

Revelation requires the response of intuition and faith in addition to the assent of reason. Yet when men of moral earnestness truly behold Jesus Christ, it is not faith nor reason alone, but direct apprehension that rises within them to declare Christ not only Son of Man, as he called himself. "Flesh and blood have not revealed this unto thee," said Christ to Peter, "but my Father which is in heaven."

The Christian answer does not exempt man from existence, nor from the anguish and responsibility of freedom; it requires both existence and responsibility of him; yet tells him the news almost too good to be true, that he is not alone. Both Christianity and Sartre require of man freedom and responsibility, but the freedom of Sartre is attached to a meaningless world. To Sartre, responsibility is a necessary value man himself has created; in Christianity, responsibility is the structure of the universe, the character of Power, Process, and Purpose, the nature of God. On Sartre's terms, however, man may not with equal legitimacy accept or invent irresponsibility as his value and live by it. Every criminal, from Hitler to common thief, accepted from others, or invented, the false values by which he lived.

My second question was another form of the first: "Is the world meaningful or meaningless?" M. Queneau replied that, to Sartre, the only meaning that exists man himself has created. Man has found no purpose in life, except to refuse slavery, to pursue freedom; he has invented every lesser purpose. This was not unlike the philosophy of John Dewey, as he explained it to me at his Manhattan apartment. Indeed, in his latest book, questions are considered better than final answers (whether Atheist or Theist, Communist, Romanist, or Capitalist), for full truth exceeds man's limited omniscience; only Reality includes, and is greater than, man.

One cannot evade the conclusion that, to Sartre, though no God exists, Man is man's God. Man is the sole creator, to whom the tribute must be given — he has created himself — a tribute which presupposes the creating intelligence which was created. This is as clear a form as can be found of what Maritain calls, "Anthropotheism." Man, who will not have God, worships himself as God. It is also a clear example of what Maritain calls "Irrationalism."

"What, therefore," I asked, "shall be regarded as the nature of morality? Shall the basis of action be absolute morality, coming to man from above and from within his own nature, or expediency, that is, enlightened self-interest?" "The sole basis of ethics," said Queneau, "in the Sartre philosophy is the fact of freedom. Therefore, whatever assists the growth of freedom is moral; whatever hinders freedom is immoral." This is, of course, the only ethical principle that could be based upon Sartre's system, and, again it must be said, here Sartre has torn an important leaf from the Book of Christ, for in Christianity also the requirements of freedom, in soul and society, are the basis of morality, with this difference: in Christianity man pursues the requirements of freedom in the presence of a moral Absolute, a holy God, whereas, in Sartre, man pursues freedom only in his own presence. And the Self in whose presence man pursues freedom, in Sartre, is a Self prior to good and evil, independent of moral demand.

"What, as Sartre and Camus see it," I asked, "is the chief end of man?" The answer was already obvious, but the question had to be put. M. Queneau replied: "The pursuit of freedom." Volumes could be written classifying the various kinds of freedom men do, in fact, pursue; adultery, individual and mass murder, the attempt of the Nordic to eliminate the Semitic race — all these principles of conduct, in Sartre's philosophy, have been created by man in pursuit of his freedom; they are, therefore, on terms of expediency, moral. Verily, freedom pursued in the vacuum of a meaningless world, that is, anarchic freedom, seems more man's enemy than his friend, and another form of idolatry. Yet Sartre himself resisted Hitler's slavery, and would, I think, resist the Russian — for the sake of freedom as an Absolute demand, something more than individual caprice. Indeed, in his view, the absolute demand for free world and free mind is present in existence itself, indeed its very essence. His God is then immanent, if not transcendent also.

In conclusion I asked: "Was Sartre reared as an atheist, a Protestant, or a Roman; has any particular event in his life influenced his thought?" "Sartre's background," Queneau replied, "has been nominal Romanism." I was reminded of Marc Boegner's remark, during my interview with him: "France is nominally

Roman and actually pagan." "One particular event of significance," Queneau continued, "was Sartre's year in a German prison camp during the last War. In this context Sartre certainly discovered at first hand some of the horrible forms of slavery which man's freedom has created. Here also Sartre discovered the theater, and for the prison stage his first plays were written."

The love of freedom, for its own sake, can understandably develop in a context of coercion. But freedom, at the demand of God, for the sake of man, is a responsible or moral freedom, an end in itself, yet also a means to enriched fellowship. Community is preferable to enmity. Indeed, an idolatry of freedom can itself produce slavery, for extremes often meet. Coercion leads to anarchy, and anarchy to coercion; Community redeems man from both.

"Has Sartre been influenced by Kierkegaard, Nietzsche, and Dostoyevsky?" I asked at parting. "Not by Kierkegaard," Queneau replied, "except as mediated by Heidegger, but he read Nietzsche in his youth and has undoubtedly been influenced by Dostoyevsky." Nietzsche's stress upon anthropotheism, upon human freedom as above morality and prior to it, is identical with Sartre's Existentialism, while Dostoyevsky's stress on freedom is similar, though in the distinct context of specific belief in a moral God and personal immortality.

Nothing is so great an enemy of Christianity as a distinct system which closely resembles it. The immemorial spirit of antichrist, abroad in Western Civilization, seems, in Sartre, disguised as an angel of light. Yet, as Etienne Gilson put it in our interview: "Sartre is a young man of great ability and vitality; he is still growing; it is not yet certain that he will not finally move on into the Christian Faith, compelled to do so by the very necessities of the freedom he values, making the transition from a meaningful freedom in a meaningless universe to a more meaningful freedom in a meaningful world."

Whether or not Sartre moves from Sartre to Christ, the philosophy he has set in motion in the world, with its existential accent on human freedom and responsibility, should help deliver us from bondage to any form of biological or naturalistic determinism on the one hand, for, in Sartre's view, science does not create man; man creates science. On the other hand, his philosophy may provide modern men with an apparent exit from the presence of responsibility through self-deification, whose final nature is the isolation of the ego, whose end product Christians have always called Hell, that is, psycho-social loneliness — in Sorokin's view, the *cause* of suicide. For suicide is, as Dostoyevsky observed, also a form of freedom; apart from God and His love, it may be the major tragic freedom — to say "No" to life.

Queneau stated that Sartre and Camus would appreciate and read copies of my Dostoyevsky (*Theology Today*) and Kierkegaard (*Religion In Life*) essays, if I should send them upon my return to America.

Expressing a profound gratitude to M. Queneau for his patience and help, and for his adequate English, I made my departure. I had not visited the temporarily inaccessible Sartre and Camus, but felt a clearer understanding of the French Existentialist "No" to any form of slavery — indeed a greater admiration, for neither Ego-Anarchy nor Collective Coercion (the Russian threat) is its purpose.

To find Gabrielle Marcel, leader of the French Christian Existentialists, I had to journey to southern France. Le Pouck appeared out of the mist, an authentic sixteenth century castle with iron-latticed windows and four foot stone walls. A lofty tower commanded the valley. To my chagrin M. Marcel was not at home, but his sister-in-law, a French gentle-woman, welcomed me with old-world grace. She had heard of me, she said, through her sister, M. Marcel's wife, whom I had met in the Swiss Alps, and explained that Marcel was expected at the chateau at eight-thirty. Tea, with French bread and jam, appeared from the huge kitchen, and Marcel's niece, Helene, an attractive maid of twenty, while waiting for M. Marcel and dinner, summarized in fair English a recent Sartre play, anti-Communist in theme.

I was privileged to examine the great collection of books which had been Marcel's father's library. I spent some time also with three of Marcel's own volumes, brought for my inspection: *Existentialisme Chretien*, its Foreword by my friend, Etienne Gilson, of the French Academy, a volume of definitive essays on Christian

Existentialism spiced with tributes to Marcel by leading French writers, published in 1917 by Librarie Plon, Les Petits-Fils de Plon et Nourrit, at No. 8, rue Garanciere, Paris VI; *Etre et Avoir,* by Marcel, issued in 1928 by Fernand Aubier at No. 13, Quai Conti, Paris; and *Des Refus a L'Invoication,* published in 1940 by Gallimard, publisher also of Sartre's volumes.

After a time I was conducted by Marcel's niece and nephew through the castle and its tower, and then, joined by my gracious hostess and Marcel's tiny grandchildren, Odile and Therese, across the valley for the milk. We walked past ancient low-roofed dwellings inhabited at one end by burly peasants, and at the other by their cattle and goats. We exchanged greetings and information with friendly farm folk, and returned to the chateau through a circuitous wooded path. At seven-thirty Gabrielle Marcel arrived, with his son, Jean Marie, as chauffeur in the Citroen, and the son's half-English, half-French friend, Gerard Mansell, on vacation from London Art School.

M. Marcel was typically French, with small white moustache and underlip goatee. He wore the inevitable French beret, was short of stature, with eyes and hands that spoke as meaningfully as his lips. An hour before dinner our conversation began, to continue after dinner till ten o'clock, and on the morrow until one.

The evening was unforgettable; one of the great minds of France, as well known in philosophy as in faith, disclosed itself to me.

I described, at M. Marcel's request, my interviews with eminent Europeans — Berdiaeff in France, Maritain in Rome, Brunner in Zurich, Toynbee in London, C. S. Lewis in Oxford, C. H. Dodd in Cambridge. It had been Berdiaeff, among many others, who had urged that I see Marcel. I told the story of my earlier efforts to see him; some of these details had been related to him by his wife and Me. Chessex. I had wanted to see him for many reasons, I explained, but among them was the desire to make his affirmative work better known in America, in whose universities the freedom-pursuing gospel of Sartre (a negation to slavery in any form) had already found welcome.

My first query concerned Marcel's spiritual biography. Unlike Sartre, who had been reared in Romanism, Marcel had been reared in freethought. His mother had been religious, but his father, well cultivated for his age, had been the moral atheist familiar to the nineteenth century. No religious training had been provided in Marcel's youth, nor in his adolescence. At four years of age his mother's death had deepened his spiritual sensitivity. From then on he had been inwardly religious, though not outwardly so. He had had no association with formal religion until 1929 when the inner development had produced an existential decision — to confess openly his Christian discipleship and join a Church. A French Christian author had written to him, during an exchange of letters on a different theme, "You think like us, why do you not join us?" Presently he had made up his mind, confessed himself a Christian, and joined the Roman Church. He had pondered for a time membership in a Protestant Church, for his wife had been of Reformed Faith. Indeed fully half his friends had been and were still Protestant. He was thoroughly in sympathy with the World Council of Churches; one of its presidents, Marc Boegner, was his cousin; he knew personally many of its leaders. He had very little patience with the then papal attitude toward the World Council, an attitude of total negation. Christian Ecumenicity, an authentic Catholicity, was a central theme in his thinking. He had decided to join the Roman Church, however, primarily because Protestants seemed of divided mind about Christianity itself. Liberal Protestants, for example, did not believe in the divinity of Christ, and were equally hazy about every central Christian idea. Among Protestants, "You never quite knew where you were."

Marcel acknowledged that there were as well deplorable Romans, representing "a nominal, external, almost purely political Catholicism." Protestantism had, in the past, greatly emphasized a central necessity in Christianity, namely, personal life in God through the Holy Spirit. This accent should never be surrendered, he said, either in Protestantism or Romanism.

I urged Marcel to define Christian Existentialism as he understood it. He explained that he had recently stated in lectures to the students who shared each Friday an *entretien* at his home, and in various published articles, that he did not insist on the word "Existentialist," which was, in itself, quite meaningless. It became meaningful only as its content became, in his view, the Sartre infra-paganism, or Christianity. An Existentialist Christian, of course, was interested not so much in conceptual theology as in theology incarnate in spiritual experience. Three ideas had been central in his thought. The first: a redefinition of the relation between *creativity* and *receptivity*. Kant had been in error, Marcel believed, in defining receptivity as mere passive acceptance of the wisdom of the past, and creativity as spontaneous, active grappling with life and truth. He, Marcel, had been at pains to point out that true receptivity, misunderstood by Kant, required in fact the most intense activity. The wisdom of the past had never been disclosed to the passive mind. The inactive mind could receive nothing, either of the past or the present. Only the active mind could either understand or appropriate the past, distinguishing its truth from its error. To consider orthodoxy dead, and heterodoxy alive, had been the major error of Kantian and post-Kantian philosophy, a basic blindness of subsequent thought. From Descartes on, every would be thinker, as his first act, had discarded the painfully acquired wisdom of man and built his philosophical system as a *de novo* creation — with the end product, solipsism. No renaissance, either in philosophy or science, could occur until the creative role of true receptivity was again recognized. Only then could modern man build upon, rather than apart from, the wisdom of the ages. Only then could mankind view in true perspective either past or present follies. From sheer *de novo* creativity, all folly appeared wisdom, all dross appeared gold.

The second pivotal idea in Marcel's thought, similar to the first, was his view of *fidelity*. It had been mistakenly assumed that faithfulness was static, involving the maintenance of received faith and wisdom exactly as received. But this assumption had overlooked the essential element of growth; true fidelity included living development. To illustrate, said Marcel: suppose a child of ten were left in your care on condition that you return him to his rightful guardian at twenty. A false idea of fidelity would cause you to restrict the child's growth in the vain endeavour to return him "exactly as received." True fidelity would return the same child, matured through ten years of normal development. Fidelity therefore included growth; it was clearly a dynamic rather than a static idea. Fidelity to the Christian tradition, an Ecumenical fellowship of men and women obedient to Christ, was not, therefore, the motionless caricature pictured by clever unbelievers. It was rather a total activity of the whole man, a living companionship with Christ the Saviour through the Holy Spirit. Growth was its major characteristic. Infidelity was the truly static concept, for it accepted passively the spiritual status quo. Various forms of self-conscious literalism had omitted dynamic growth from fidelity, while equally self-conscious liberalism had omitted fidelity altogether. Between literalism and liberalism lay the Christian tradition, receptively creative, and dynamically faithful.

The third focal emphasis in Marcel's thought was *Incarnation* —not alone "the Word made flesh" but the incarnation of idea in practice, of spirit in body, of love in life. This principle is similar to Sartre's idea of *Involvement,* and is naturally basic in any Existentialism, Christian or atheist. But Marcel carries the principle a step farther. He was interested, he said, in the idea that our bodies and our spirits are not wholly separable, that even our bodies partake of spiritual reality. The atheist looks toward death as the end through his materialization of the spirit; but the Christian looks toward immortality, however understood, as the end through his spiritualization of the body. On what other grounds could Christ's resurrection be explicable, or the Christian hope, as the Creed has it, of the resurrection of the body?

In opposition to Sartre's idea that existence precedes essence, Marcel stated, as Etienne Gilson had done, in our interview, that *essence precedes existence.* That is, said Marcel, existence of itself has no meaning; it receives its meaning from essence. You could illustrate the principle thus, said he: the earth would be uninhabitable darkness but for the light shining upon it from above, and the light is precisely that upon which light can not be shed, since it is itself the Source of light.

It is Gilson who has described Marcel as, at one and the same time, "authentically existentialist and authentically Christian."

Marcel acknowledged himself closer to Gilson than to Maritain, to neo-Platonism than to Thomism, emphasizing direct fellowship with Christ by the Spirit rather than an hierarchical Church and an hierarchical structure of science, philosophy, and theology. Moving from Christian Existentialism *per se* to its social implications, I enquired: "What of the conflicts between races and classes?" Marcel had uniformly opposed racism in all its forms, he said. He believed that the Christian society which gave house room to racial discrimination was in large part pagan. On the issue of class, and the pursuit of a classless society, Marcel emphasized that equality and fraternity were irreconcilable concepts — for equality seemed rooted in envy and egoism, while fraternity was rooted in charity. An externally coerced equality was not fraternity. As a matter of fact, it had proven itself the enemy of fraternity, in recent Russian history, where the original notion of equality had been gradually transformed in practice into the most grotesque inequality. The best situation was one in which snobbery, hidden or open, did not exist, where men were unconscious of class distinctions — because they issued from natural differences of ability within a familial community. The French system of titled nobility, said Marcel, though now a name rather than a power, contained a hidden snobbery painfully obvious to everyone. Aristocracies of money, like those of birth, similarly missed the familial basis of fellowship, in which natural differences of ability in labor and leadership arose in freedom and were accepted unconsciously.

Politically, said Marcel, he had long urged a United States of Europe. Imponderable social forces, among them the heavy consciousness of national and local history, retarded the good achievement. The U. N. O. would certainly break down if it proved a society of national egoists; it could live as a creative endeavour only in an atmosphere of fraternity, essentially heterocentric rather than egocentric in character. Communism in Russia had given way to totalitarianism's police state, and coercion rather than community, a regime of force and fraud rather than a fellowship of kindred minds, had developed an all-powerful bureaucracy, forever the enemy of true creativity. God was always on the side of creativity; bureaucracy, or *etatisme,* was forever a dead hand upon creativity, and represented not only the end of freedom but also the end of hope.

What of the concept of freedom? I asked. As the word was understood by many moderns, particularly of the Sartre school, said Marcel, freedom meant anarchy. Anarchy was, at bottom, the Sartre philosophy, though the unpopular word was not used. Absolute solipsism and anarchic egoism, basically identical, were strong in contemporary thought. Christian freedom was to be understood as fraternal creativity. As fraternal creativity died in the souls of men, Eastern Communism claimed the moribund residuum. Coercive economies, of all sorts, came to power only when creativity was dead. Marcel planned to stress this and other themes in his scheduled lectures, on the Gifford Foundation, at the University of Aberdeen.

The relationship between freedom and necessity had been widely misunderstood in recent years, notably in Sartre's philosophy, said Marcel. Sartre believed the significance of man lay in freedom, yet some of man's significance lay also in necessity. Men were seldom at their best when poised in anguish between two decisions; rather they were often at their best when they were laboring at an assignment, or following a course of action, upon which a decision had already been made. Every man knew that he experienced his greatest sense of freedom when he was busily in pursuit of settled objectives, when he was thus in the control of necessity, and his greatest sense of unfreedom when halting between two opinions. The creative role of necessity in human life, and in the human spirit, had been underestimated in much of modern thought. The fact that man was as much a creature of necessity as of freedom was not an evil but a good, for it formed the basis of his sanity. When men were forced endlessly to decide and re-decide, on every issue of thought and action, complete mental breakdown was not far away. Health in mind and society depended on good habits, that is, actions which had passed from the battleground of freedom to the parade ground of necessity. Absolute freedom was as unthinkable as absolute necessity. Man at his best was both free and not free. The best society therefore corresponded with the truest view of human nature. If society operated only on the basis of freedom, as advocated by Sartre, it would be an intolerable anarchy; if it operated only on the basis of necessity, it would prove an intolerable tyranny. A middle ground might be found between Russia and America, but, to be acceptable to Christians, it would have to be a socialized commonwealth which served rather than obstructed free creativity. Marcel's thought at this point, I suggested, was identical with Nicholas Berdiaeff's concept of *Sobornst* — a community of love and freedom, rather than a collective coercion.

America, I explained, quoting Toynbee, was a generation or two behind Europe intellectually and theologically, though ahead of Europe in the mass manufacture of gadgets. Marcel replied: "But Europe is a generation or two behind itself. Sartre's philosophy, for example, is not a return to paganism, for the pagans were always both religious and moral in basic presuppositions. Sartre's philosophy is therefore infra-pagan, not a return to paganism but a drop beneath it. Europe's problem is to catch up with itself, to keep abreast of its own Christian creativity."

The intellectual Battle of Paris, between the affirmative Existentialism of Marcel and the negative Existentialism of Sartre, though the second is a negation to slavery for the sake of freedom, is not a merely local engagement, but a basic Battle in the soul of the West, possibly (under cover) in Russia itself.

Marcel was not of one mind with our mutual friend, Nicholas Berdiaeff, who had said to me that "catastrophe" would prove the strongest factor in bringing about Western spiritual recovery. Marcel was deeply moved by a general de-Christianization alongside spiritual renewal. Spiritual recovery, in his opinion, sometimes occurred in spite of calamity. Nothing could have been more catastrophic than the last two Wars, yet while intellectuals, peasants, and laborers had joined the creative minority, a numerical majority had experienced further moral and spiritual decline. In particular, Marcel was deeply moved by a General de-Christianization among French peasants.

What did I think, Marcel asked, about the future of Western Civilization? It seemed to me, I said, that it is the way of civilizations to tend to nothing, unless caught up and transfigured by something greater than themselves. At the beginning they grow as they are produced by spiritually creative minorities. When they grow away from their creative principle, as the West seems, perhaps superficially, to have grown away from Christ, their creative period is over. Various coercive economies gather up the debris for a time to stall off extinction. Yet as a civilization disintegrates, a minority, what the prophets of Israel called "The Lord's Remnant," rediscovers its creative Faith. Around this creative minority a new civilization rises from the ashes of the old. Today, Russia seems like the Roman Empire under the Caesars, and from its decline the Christian minority will build anew. Perhaps Russia is even more like Nebuchadnezzar's Chaldean Empire, raised as the lash of the Lord to scourge a spiritually slumbering Israel.

"Stalin and his successors seem more like Nebuchadnezzar than Caesar," said Marcel in agreement, "for in Rome freedom existed within law."

It was clear that Marcel, like many another Christian prophet of our time, is an agent of the Vox Dei, offering Free Minds in the Free World an escape from the threatening paralysis of bureaucracy, whether Eastern or Western, through a recovery of an eternally available, eternally contemporary, creativity.

THE RUSSIAN ORTHODOX POINT OF VIEW

NICHOLAS BERDIAEFF

I was first introduced to the mind of N. Berdiaeff during my study for the doctorate in philosophy at Drew University. The cosmopolitan leadership of the eminent Christian classicist, Stanley Romaine Hopper, then Associate Professor to the colourful Lynn Harold Hough, proved immensely stimulating. N. Berdiaeff came often into our classroom discussions, and was continually called to our attention in research assignments. At first this Russian exile in Paris seemed merely exotic, but as time wore on his dialectical skill, and the penetration of his ideas, won my deep respect. At the time I was slowly and painfully emerging from ten years of atheism into faith, and I was wholesomely impressed by what appeared a truly great mind among Christian writers.

A year or two later I ran into N. Berdiaeff again while seeking a pattern of dominant Christian beliefs among contemporary voices. His tremendous emphasis on the vitality of the Spirit, playing its regenerating role in history, quite fascinated me. In particular, in view of my recent secular mentality, not wholly forgotten though departed, I was struck by his idea that man was not made to receive life *from* society; it was *to* society that a man was the vessel of life. Not long ago, while reading Toynbee's volumes, I found this idea reiterated with power.

Still later, N. Berdiaeff's name came again to the fore at an annual meeting of the Southern Society for the Philosophy of Religion near Asheville, N. C. A paper was read on Berdiaeff's three-level conception of time — calendar or cosmic or circular time, historic or human time, and deep time or eternity. All social and personal resurrection resulted from some impingement of deep time or eternity upon historic or human time. The idea produced a remarkable effect upon the assembled teachers of philosophy and religion from scattered southern colleges and universities; a marked line of division immediately appeared separating the deistic or agnostic or atheistic goats from the theistic sheep. At the same session I quoted repeatedly from Berdiaeff's book on Dostoyevsky in the presentation of my essay on the metaphysical Russian novelist.

It is understandable then that I anticipated with the keenest pleasure a discussion of Christianity's current, or recurrent, problems with N. Berdiaeff in person. It was approximately three o'clock on a Friday afternoon when I reached Paris; the same evening at seven I was at his home in Clamart. Much to my chagrin the house-keeper informed me, across the mist of our common language limitations, that he was gone for his health to a watering place called Chatel Guyon, two or three hundred kilometres south of Paris. Very graciously she provided me with his exact address. It had not been possible to arrange an appointment for three reasons: I had not known his address beyond the fact that he was, or had been, director of the Academy for the Philosophy of Religion in Paris; I had no exact information from the United States Lines about the hour, or even the day, of arrival; and it would have been highly presumptuous to have expected N. Berdiaeff to rearrange any part of his summer schedule to suit my convenience. A great mind, like a falcon, is best photographed "on the wing."

Sunday morning, approximately forty hours after I had reached Paris, I presented myself at the Hotel L'Etablissement in Chatel Guyon; within a few minutes Nicholas Berdiaeff stood before me. I was reminded at once of photographs of the elderly Mark Twain, though N. Berdiaeff's hair was gray rather than white. There was a ruggedness about his face, and an unmistakable gentleness in his eyes.

N. Berdiaeff speaks three languages but no English, and his French has a decided Russian accent. It was clear that our con-versation would be brief without assistance. A handsome French veteran, M. R. Perriere from Oran, Algeria, came at once to our aid. Accustomed only to military terminology as interpreter in the

War, he found the vocabulary of philosophy and religion peculiarly difficult, but made up in graciousness of spirit for any other shortcoming. Occasionally our three-cornered conversation broke down in laughter over translation incongruities.

It was a Sunday morning to be cherished. We began by discussing Dostoyevsky briefly, then passed quickly to my friend Sorokin of Harvard. N. Berdiaeff had known Sorokin, though not intimately, during the rugged days of the Russian Revolution, when both had served in the Kerensky Government. He was pleased that Sorokin had, like himself, moved away from Secularism, or Sensatism. I described in brief my reading of Sorokin and my interviews with him. He had not known that Sorokin, like himself, had been exiled from Russia by the Bolshevik Government. I gave also the history of my acquaintance with the name of Berdiaeff.

Before many minutes had passed present-day Russian-American relations had entered our conversation. He asked whether the American people desired war with Russia. I replied that the answer to that question was necessarily two-fold: the American people saw no cause for war with the Russian people; they had no yearning whatever for war with any one. At the same time the American people saw little basis for peace with the present Russian regime. The Russian one-party government sought to push its way through a democratic world whose very terminology was a foreign language. Totalitarian Communism was not tolerable in the Free World. N. Berdiaeff was pleased that good will existed between the peoples of the two countries. War did not seem to him inevitable even in view of Russia's inability to understand parliamentary procedure. N. Berdiaeff regarded Russian Communism, even in its present modified state, as a particularly virulent form of materialistic Collectivism — a mechanistic regime superimposed by brute force, cancelling at once both spirituality and liberty. He expressed the hopeful opinion, however, that Russia did not desire further land expansion, as the Nazis had done, but merely a buffer-circle of friendly, that is, communistic, Powers.

This is, of course, an important distinction, if it is true, for Russia seems possessed of ample "Living Space," while Hitler could, and did, shout the point effectively to Germans. Russia has plenty of land area, while the Nazi land area was limited. Russia may desire only to live in peace while she consolidates her Resources and her people. It is possible that this is true; it is well if this is true. With vast areas of land as yet undigested, the Russian Python may have no wish to swallow more. I pointed out, however, that totalitarian states, dominated by single parties denying their critics the right to be heard, normally have every power except that of self-restraint. Irving Babbitt was at pains to describe the inevitable absence of an "Inner Check" in all single-party governments. Without the gift of self-control, what could a tyranny do but seek further expansion? In any case, there is hope, whether false or true, in the idea that Russia at this time may desire only an opportunity to put her own large house in order. Call it wishful thinking, or what you will, but as long as doubt remains concerning a runaway Russian expansionism, there seems insufficient reason for war. The policy of the United Nations, and of John F. Kennedy — be ready, but if war starts, let Russia start it — seems the right one, perhaps the only possible one to folk who would lead the way to creative peace.

I sought N. Berdiaeff's estimate of the French Existentialists. He was sad that Sartre and his kind had been influenced by Heidegger rather than by Kierkegaard, and that, while Sartre was opposed to collectivism, his point of departure seemed identical with Marxian materialism, recognizing no Meaning in the Universe except its own. The existentialism of Sartre seemed atheism simply, without the grace of originality — an endeavour to glorify solipsism as the law for man. Sartre, in thumb-nail description, was a Twentieth Century Nietzsche with a French accent. To an American Sartre might appear with equal accuracy as a French John Dewey turned inside out — a solipsistic rather than an altruistic atheist. The moral law, like scientific law, as something mankind did not invent but discovered, having nothing in common with expediency as a mask for deified self-interest, in Sartre as in Nietzsche and Dewey, was not but seemed voted out of existence. Yet the pursuit of political and personal freedom *is* moral; it is bondage that is *immoral,* against which Sartre says "No." It is not the name, but the fact, of freedom from bondage which is important, on Christian terms, to God and man.

N. Berdiaeff described with admiration the Marcel Existentialists in France. They were less well known, for the same reason that good news seldom made headlines. The existentialism of Gabrielle Marcel was as different from the solipsism of Sartre as day is different from night. Marcel sees modern man at a crossroads of decision: he may continue to deify himself, when man is *obviously* not the Father but the Child, and further the overall catastrophe, or he may enter again the freedom and faithfulness of fellowship, to share a new, and true, resurrection.

N. Berdiaeff asked if I had heard of an American writer, Reinhold Niebuhr. I explained that Niebuhr's paradoxical position was too orthodox for secularists and too socialistic for conservatives; I then summarized the Niebuhr answers to my questions in our interview. Russian Orthodox in denomination, and, like all Thomists, a structural thinker, N. Berdiaeff seemed closer to Romanism than Niebuhr. Berdiaeff expressed deep admiration for Maritain.

What could be done to aid in Protestantism's recovery as an instrument of Power and Grace? Naturally enough, there was no ready answer to such a question. Thinking nation-wise for a moment, N. Berdiaeff saw little hope for a numerical triumph of Evangelical Christianity in modern Russia. A deeper and more significant triumph was the Christian deepening among the Russian minority. (Christianity itself, as Toynbee puts it, arose in the Roman minority, and lived to create a new society after Rome's decline and fall.) In France, Nicholas Berdiaeff saw a real opportunity for Protestant growth, for the French Reformed Church possessed classical Christianity and cultural breadth, as well as the sympathy of the populace. He did not know, he said, a great deal about American Protestantism, beyond its Puritan beginnings. I informed him that I had heard of Puritans but had never met one in the flesh; that the last one, according to Santayana, had died by his own hand. My own denomination, the Methodist Church, I explained, had been characterized as Puritanism's last stand. N. Berdiaeff was convinced that Protestant Christianity, not having Rome's authoritarian organization, could neither compete with Rome nor extend its own domain without a serious commitment to the Faith of Calvin and Luther as well as of Francis of Assisi, Augustine, and the Martyrs. Unless modern Christians believed in Christianity, why indeed should they support it at all? If they believed only negatively, not having adopted another positive religion, they should remember that the Marxian and Nazi experiments have failed to be convincing substitutes. Would it not be well for Protestant Christians to *believe* their beliefs, to take Christ seriously as a Great Prophet, a Son of Man, and Greater than a Prophet, the Son of God, the Divine Light and Sacrifice for Mankind?

Did I have any evidence, N. Berdiaeff asked, that American Protestantism was not whole-hearted about its commitment to classical Christianity? I confessed that my evidence was not statistical, not of the Gallup-poll variety; it was rather an estimate based on surface acquaintance. Protestantism had found a numerical stronghold in America, I asserted, but confusion about the nature of Christianity was often present — perhaps a normal blight upon a healthy organism. I myself would defend the view with emphasis that American Protestantism has its five thousand that have not bowed the knee to Solipsism, Relativism, or Fundamentalism, who continue steadfastly to worship Christ as God's gift for human resurrection. I would say further that American Protestantism has no disease that Central Christianity, given half a chance, would not cure. The need is obvious — the bold proclamation of Christ, that men might live in Love, that Love might live in men.

German Protestantism could not be accused of cultural obscurantism, N. Berdiaeff explained, for it had taken the lead in scientific advance and the "higher criticism" of the Bible. If anything, it had gone too far in its supine surrender to, rather than fellowship with, and use of, the scientific method. German Protestantism had not been Fundamentalism, for Christ, and not the Bible, had been the object of its worship. Men like Pastor Niemoeller had been the German Protestant leaders. Political expediency had moved Christ into second place among others who readily paid lip-service to Hitler.

What single thing, I asked, would prove most effective in curing Protestantism, or for that matter the whole of Christendom, from whatever faithlessness existed at its heart? N. Berdiaeff answered with one word: "Catastrophe." We are living, he said, in the very midst of an overall catastrophe so huge that we are unaware of its existence only because we are on the inside of it. The successive military explosions of this century are mere bubbles on the surface of the boiling cauldron of catastrophe. This catastrophe is the harvest of man's long sowing to unbelief and egoism, his annihilation of God in his heart, his deification of self, his worship of the secondary, his denial of the primary. The harvest is not yet ended, for we have not yet experienced the full judgment of God, whose powerful hand is restrained that we may not perish. Hope exists in the faith that at "the end of the end" of sorrow and despair, repentant and chastened men, and forgiving and renewing God will create, beyond catastrophe and chaos, a new beginning, a new heaven, a new earth, a new (and the first) World Community.

I was impressed that N. Berdiaeff was in profound agreement with Sorokin and Toynbee on this point. Indeed, not long ago (Christmas, 1961), a personal letter from Sorokin, describing his recent European conference with Mr. and Mrs. Toynbee, disclosed their reaching, after long difference, essential agreement.

The concluding theme of our conversation concerned Collectivism, Community, and Liberty. It was possible, said the Prophet in Exile, to maintain a true balance between Community and Liberty, for Community received its authority from the consciences of men. However, great stress had to be placed upon common responsibility for the solution of common problems. Responsibility did not exist unless it existed within individual men. Community, like law, was the conscience of individual men; without it liberty quickly disintegrated into anarchy. The Creator of Community was the Church, he said, when the Church was in full vigour as the Body of the Holy Spirit. Without spiritual vitality Community dissolved into Collectivism or Anarchy. The Church, as the Community of Faith, was forever opposed to the Collectivism of Force. Members of Christ's Church, across all the living branches of the Great Tree, were united around a common discipline which they had accepted without coercion. The only possible rescue of Community from Collectivism and Anarchy had to come through a resurrection of spiritual vitality in Christ's Church.

Collectivism, which offered a pseudo-community, was the enemy alike of true Community and true Liberty. Superimposed by force of arms, Collectivism was mechanical and not spiritual, an organization only and not an organism. Regarding itself as above the moral law, it would be crushed below it, the foe of true humanity and true Divinity.

Community meant Liberty-within-Law, and rested finally upon Law-within-men. Democracy tended to fall apart into egoistic Anarchy on the one hand or bureaucratic Collectivism on the other, but at its best offered a true balance between social action and individual freedom. Community was an organism, a living society in which Liberty could breathe; Collectivism and Anarchy were the opposite extremes which always proved to be two names for one thing. N. Berdiaeff was in process of writing a new volume concerning this theme.

With all his interests, Nicholas Berdiaeff seemed nonetheless a lonely man. He deeply mourned the passing of his beloved wife but two years before. Not a young man (he was born in 1874 in Russia), he was fully himself, clear of mind, strong in faith, a father to the faithful.

THE ENGLISH CONGREGATIONAL
POINT OF VIEW

NATHANIEL MICKLEM

A few years ago I was deeply stirred by Nathaniel Micklem's book, *The Theology of Politics*. As the title suggests, Micklem had developed the thesis: "Every political problem is at bottom theological." This truth was perhaps always self-evident to the discriminating, but today, after two world wars, facing the threat of another, is it not clear also to the man on the street? Bad metaphysics produced Hitler and his bloodthirsty race-worshippers; bad theology created Marxian materialism and class antagonism. Better theology chose the lesser of two evils, to obstruct rather than to appease Hitlerism.

An expectant spirit quickened my pace as I walked from Oxford's Eastgate Hotel, following luncheon with Professor Gwyn Jones of the University of Wales, past the Bodlean Library, where I had completed further research in Toynbee, right toward New College, and left beyond Manchester to Mansfield's spacious grounds.[1] I found the Mansfield Principal enjoying his pipe in a lawn swing by the garden. He was reading George Santayana's sadly disbelieving but sympathetic *The Christ Of The Gospels*. He breathed the spirit of cordiality, and was as pleased that I had appreciated his volume as he was amused that I considered him a major prophet.

We came at once to the question: "What exactly hinders harmony between Thomism and Personalism, or between Protestantism and Romanism — or, if you like, between Reason and Romanticism?"

1. Later, on another visit to England, I gave the lectures at Manchester which became my book, *Epistle to the Skeptics,* and two sets at Mansfield, my *Major Voices in American Theology* and *Men Who Shape Belief;* to Mansfield, the Fall of 1964, I am committed to return (to lecture on the Twentieth Century Relevance of Man's Major Religions).

There was more common ground, said Mr. Micklem, between opposed philosophies than between opposed Communions. The Roman hierarchy, in Spain, Mexico, and the Philippines, had demonstrated its thorough intractability, its complete totalitarianism, its undeviating support of the classes against the masses. Nothing whatever, apparently, could be done, he said, but to resist Roman authoritarianism as one resisted Nazi, Fascist, and Marxist despotisms. Yet the papal encyclicals, if one could tell what was meant by the phrase "corporate state", had seemed enlightened enough.

It was desirable that unity be restored in Christendom, that political and economic unity might possess a soul, but a meeting of Roman and Protestant minds, Micklem stated, would probably long precede a meeting of hierarchies. The notion of papal infallibility had made it as impossible for the Pope, as for Stalin-and-successors, he said, to understand democratic diplomacy. The free expression of differences, toward better fellowship between equals, to an absolute autocrat was meaningless.

The major need of our generation, Micklem asserted, was a genuine religious awakening. No moral or spiritual regeneration in history had proceeded from an ecclesiastical hierarchy, last to comprehend new Life among the people. New Life was the desperate need of the hour. There had been some shattering of central Christianity in England, though considerably less than in America, but the Christian message was everywhere welcomed. A genuine religious awakening would cure the intellectual, and moral, backsliding of our time. A renewal of Spirit and Power could not come to pass until men were obedient to the Word of Christ as God and Saviour. Barth and Brunner had underscored the only intellectual basis for revival, the Word of God. If received with high seriousness, the Word was the Creator of Life.

Nothing, said Micklem, could be built on the absence of profound conviction. The Christianity which had given birth to Western Civilization had received its Power from the regenerating Faith that God was in Christ reconciling the World unto Himself. In the Word of Christ God summoned men to repentance and love. The popular recovery of central Christian beliefs would produce social and spiritual resurrection; nothing else would prove of sufficient power.

The quickening of the human spirit by the Divine Spirit could not come until men hungered and thirsted after righteousness, and sought the grace of God with earnestness. A handful of genuine believers, as history had abundantly demonstrated, could always create a new society. The many would not follow until they were led by the convinced few, who had heard the Voice of Christ, had made genuine surrender to the Author of Liberty. Only with consecrated minorities would God perform His social surgery.

Central or classical Christianity had not been completely shattered, he added, even in the United States, where the emphasis was upon muscles rather than upon minds. Actually, when one considered known Trinitarians at Drew and Princeton and Union, at Yale and Toronto and Harvard, indeed at Chicago, one became aware that Christianity was not at all a lost American Cause. It was rather a Cause rediscovered. Everywhere in the States an articulate advance guard proclaimed, with John the Baptist, the Day of the Lord. The Voices hailing the new Dawn were not bewildered. Unlike the Relativists, the new leaders did not greet the age with a mouthful of negatives. They were not uncertain, like the pastors and people of the nineteenth century who went sadly through the motions of religion, believing that God had been slain by the Darwinians, and they were attending His funeral. Deism, with its dubious Deity, would no doubt continue to give the human spirit a stone rather than a song, to place its millstone about human Hopes and cast them into the sea. Not far, however, from the broad road leading to destruction there was still the narrow road leading to Life.

Christianity, in Micklem's estimation, did not prevent a left in politics. Christian social planning balanced the needs of the Community with the interests of Liberty. England might properly go further left than she had yet gone. One significant phase of planning had to be included — planning for freedom. Spiritual freedom, if taken for granted, could easily be lost. If modern attention were given exclusively to economic and political planning, spiritual freedom would certainly submerge. Planning for spiritual freedom was even more necessary than planning for economic security. A calm

119

look at pre-war Europe disclosed that in totalitarian States an all-absorbing preoccupation with economics and politics had eclipsed interest in religion and morality. The lesser work of economic planning had to be done with competence and responsibility; the greater work of spiritual planning could not be left undone. A Christian might vote on specific issues with the secular Socialists, but he had to think first of spiritual necessities. English Labor had always been religious; though less so in recent years, it still numbered thoughtful Christians among its leaders. In America, he said, a sharp division existed between secular Socialism and Christian Capitalism. The problem was therefore different, though not beyond a Christian solution. If American Christianity had abandoned Labor to Communism, was it not high time to reclaim the Foundling, and rear her in the nurture and admonition of the Lord?

Russia, and indeed Russia's fifth column in every nation, the Communist labor agitators, necessitated a policy of perpetual vigilance, of realistic resistance. An English Communist gave lip-service to England, but was actually obedient to directives from Moscow. If Russia insisted upon war, believing herself the object of Allied persecution, war would have to come, even though in that event Western Civilization might not survive. One could but choose death to tyranny, and trust God for resurrection. The democracies had to feed Europe, lest through malnutrition it succumb to the cancer of Communism. An Allied policy toward Russia of "infinite firmness plus infinite patience" had to forbear the weakness of appeasement and deal realistically with Red aggression in Eastern Europe and beyond.

C. H. DODD

T. S. Eliot had mentioned to me the name of C. H. Dodd, commending him as an excellent representative of a vigorous and articulate group of English Congregational theologians who, with great distinction, had re-asserted central Christianity. I was interested in Dodd on my own account, because his classical Christian vitality had seemed considerably more characteristic of English than of American Congregationalism. In any case, as is true of other American denominations, there are, as an historical development, two distinct Congregationalisms — one Evangelical, the other Unitarian. New England Congregationalism gained a nominal victory in the eighteenth and nineteenth centuries; the outcome, at times, seems less certain today.

Reginald Kissack, minister of Oxford's Wesley Memorial Church, Methodism's University Center, who had made it possible for me to occupy his pulpit and, with true English hospitality, had invited me on more than one occasion to his home, had similarly spoken with high praise of C. H. Dodd, regarding him of less renown but of more importance than Barth or Brunner. Another English Methodist clergyman had spoken of Dodd as "England's most significant theologian." "Though small of stature," he had said, "he is our biggest man."

I had but just returned to my hosts, the Eldreds, at Oxford, from Mrs. John Baillie's hospitality at the University of Edinburgh. Embarking upon another pilgrimage, at this point, made no great appeal. However, anticipating the stimulation of a noble mind, I set out for the Cambridge University Divinity School and Mr. Dodd.

My taxi deposited me in the rain at 3 Park Terrace; presently a charming young woman led me into a modest study. After a few moments C. H. Dodd entered, and with unassumed good cheer made me quite at home. It is probable that Mr. Dodd is not a great deal taller than the Biblical Zacchaeus, but like him he has certainly climbed into a Sycamore tree and seen the Lord. He is actively engaged in returning to mankind fourfold the Faith that others have stolen; more than half his intellectual treasures he has given to the poor in spirit.

It is possibly a doubtful compliment, but two men on my journey reminded me strongly, though only in cast of countenance, of our then American President, Mr. Truman — His Holiness Pope Pius XII and C. H. Dodd.

I was particularly anxious to learn what streams of influence had been flowing most noticeably into the river of English Congregationalism. Mr. Dodd asserted that the Thomist influence was practically non-existent or at most negligible, that Kierkegaardian

Existentialism was not strong except as mediated through Karl Barth. Barth was remarkably well represented in the English writer Jenkins, though less popular generally than Brunner. The American Niebuhrs, at Union and at Yale, were also influential.

"Was there an appreciable degree of Christian Humanism?" I asked. The term apparently had a different meaning in England than in America, for Mr. Dodd understood the question as a reference to English Unitarianism — a significant fact in itself. There was, in Dodd's opinion, little Unitarian humanism current in English religious thought. Theological Unitarianism, he said, had simply made no significant headway in England. When I explained that by the term "Christian Humanism" I meant the essential position of T. S. Eliot, uniting "the best that had been thought and said" by men with the Self-Revelation of God in Jesus Christ, Mr. Dodd asserted that there was considerably less of this influence than there ought to be. Where the position was understood, however, great sympathy for it existed. It was clear from the discussion that English Congregationalism was simply a vital development of central Christianity with an English accent, aware of common ground with all Christian Communions, but dependent not so much upon men as upon God. The strongest foreign influence was from Brunner, with a secondary penetration from Barth.

I was impressed that English Congregationalism, like all things English, contained balance. It was vigorously and primarily centered in a Deity Who was God indeed. At the same time it was not unconscious of human freedom, purpose, and responsibility.

There was not, in Dodd's opinion, anything like the interest that ought to exist, and that he himself had perpetually sought to evoke, in the World Council of Churches, among British Congregationalists. This attitude, however, did not arise from any basic disagreement with the defining Faith of the World Council, but rather from the lack of a sense of need for Ecumenical unity. Congregationalism in England believed itself a healthy Branch of the Christian Tree, was aware of its fundamental union with all Christian Communions through its commitment to Christ as God and Saviour and its share in the vitality of the Holy Spirit. There was no urgency about Ecumenicity. This seemed both natural and legitimate, for surely a growing branch was something on its own account, and probably experienced little sorrow that it was distinct from other branches. Only an inferiority mentality, entirely foreign to the spirit of Christianity, would make one Communion feel useless and helpless alone. Nonetheless, in Dodd's opinion, contemporary secularism, Marxism, and relativism demanded a united Christian Front, a non-Roman but truly Catholic Faith and Order; the World Council clearly offered this needed Christian Ecumenicity. There was no English interest whatever, he said, in the Unitarian World Alliance for Friendship Among the Churches, which had attempted to unite religious groups around the elimination of the centrality of Christ. British Congregationalism believed firmly in the Deity and in the Humanity of Jesus, and in the Life of the Holy Spirit in Church and disciple. Thus the common ground already existed for fellowship with all other central Christian denominations. The fissiparous drive of English Nonconformism had largely given way to a mood of obedience to Christ's prayer, "That they all may be one," — in obedience also to the Apostolic commandment, "Love one another, for love is of God. He that loveth not, knoweth not God, for God is Love."

Could we carry the principle one step further, I enquired, and restore in parliamentary fashion the broken union with Rome? Dodd was of the conviction that external union with Rome was not at present even a remote possibility, for the Roman emphasis upon papal absolutism had severed Roman Christians hopelessly from the total Christian Community. Reunion with Rome would have been possible if in 1870 the then reigning Pontiff had had the courage to undo the nefarious work of the Council of Trent and openly acknowledge papal subjection to a General Council. Rome's serious problem lay in the fact that it could never acknowledge an error. The Pope could do no wrong; he was amenable to no one, having renounced the superior authority of an Ecumenical Council. Therefore, he could never correct a mistake. A hierarchy that could do no wrong was an archaic and oriental despotism having nothing whatever in common with the New Testament which commanded that disciples freely confess their faults to one another and to God. An organization that could not change was not alive, and precisely speaking, he said, the Roman hierarchy and Rigor Mortis were one and the same thing. External reunion between Protestantism and Romanism could only come about by a papal acknowledgement of the superior authority of an Ecumenical Council.

Nonetheless a real union, of charity and ideology, did in fact exist between representative theologians of both Libertarian and Authoritarian Christendoms. As C. S. Lewis had suggested, this meeting of minds might well lead to eventual objective reunion, though hierarchies would of course be the last either to be aware of reunion or approve of it.

What, then, could be done, of a specific and practical nature, I enquired, to reintroduce central Christianity into any part of Christendom where it had been lost or mislaid? Dodd cited the great practical utility of the British Broadcasting Company in the Christian education of England. Bad as the situation undoubtedly was, with indifference or at least absenteeism strong among English people, it would have been infinitely worse had the BBC not provided, with remarkable continuity of purpose, that only central Christian voices, neither Fundamentalist nor Unitarian, had been heard. BBC speakers had represented Romanism and all varieties of Evangelical Protestantism, yet without exception had been chosen to present central Christianity to the people. The various religious relativisms, serving as ersatz substitutes for Christianity in America, thus had not been broadcast in England.

This use of radio for essential Christian Evangelism is typically English. Certain it is that anything like a comparable continuity of presentation, measured temporally or ideologically, simply does not exist in American broadcasting. With notable exceptions, voices seem granted continuous time, rather because of their Pied Piper charm, than because they represent central Christianity.

Preaching and prayer, with great dependence upon the Guidance and Power of the Holy Spirit, and with the liberal use of the intelligence for surmounting stubborn obstacles, clearly offered, in Dodd's opinion, the only possible avenues of effective Christian penetration into the mass American mind. There was no easy road to victory. Disintegration would increase, both extensively and intensively on the one hand, but on the other a new integration would assuredly grow. Indeed the new renaissance of central Christian Faith was already in progress in America — in Calhoun of Yale, in the two Niebuhrs, in Lewis and Hough of Drew, in many Princeton leaders, at the University of Chicago and at Harvard. The Great Light had not only not completely failed in America; as a matter of fact, it had been coming to new brilliance. Central Christianity, chastened and humbled after its nineteenth century ordeal by fundamentalism versus rationalism and the reverse, and its twentieth century ordeal by relativism, was finding itself on firm ground and in possession of increased powers.

In the political world Dodd believed that Christianity did not, after all, offer blueprints of specific measures, either economic or governmental. Christianity was rather the Critic, surveying the scene and demanding that individual liberty, as well as the claims of the community, be provided for — demanding also that statesmen abide by their promises, eschew political lying and deceit, and seek solutions rather than doctrinaire panaceas. Christianity would allow no political trespassing upon the sanctity of the individual soul. Any attempt on the part of social engineers to put a straitjacket on the human spirit would have to be resisted to the death. Social planning was, of course, a necessity, particularly in a time of shortages, but it was never intended to be more than a servant, enabling human strength to assert itself and human wisdom to apply itself to the solution of human problems. There was no substitute for human responsibility; social planning was at best merely a community expression of personal responsibility. England would have to find moral ways to solve her economic problem; minorities would continually have to be defended from majorities. British Socialism was doing a fair job in the Distribution of existing resources, through rations and queues, but was making a bad mess of Production, substituting fewer hours and higher wages for "more work".

Christianity, asserted Dodd, ever demanded moral solutions to practical problems with Divine Charity — responsibility expressed in deeds.

THE ENGLISH METHODIST POINT OF VIEW

DONALD O. SOPER

One is always interested in a distinguished bearer of his own name, and though Donald O. Soper of Kingsway Hall, London, is no traceable relation of mine, I had heard enough of his unusual leadership to wish to look him up. Englishmen, traveling in the States, had asked if I were related to London's Donald Soper, and had uniformly regaled me with striking accounts of his achievements. He was, according to reports, an effective radio preacher, a colorful Hyde Park orator able to hold a crowd, director of the West London Mission extending service through a cluster of community activities, organizer of a unique campaign, Wyclif-fashion, to take the Church to the masses, a project involving three hundred lay and ordained preachers working together among the people. Further, he was an inspirer of young men and women.

At my Knightsbridge hotel the doorman, asked the direction to Kingsway Hall, immediately responded: "O yes, that's where Dr. Soper preaches. He's a mighty fine man, interested in the people. He's doing a lot for London. I've heard him on the wireless in the program, 'Talking With You'." It is possible that hotel doormen in John Wesley's time spoke with similar appreciation of a Churchman "going forth to the people."

We met in the vestry of the West London Mission, a few minutes before morning worship. Dr. Soper's Sabbath had begun with Holy Communion, and with the day's full schedule on his mind he was nonetheless prepared to chat unhurriedly, as is the way with the English, to enquire concerning my living accommodations, and to schedule our formal interview at five in the afternoon.

126

Two things in particular impressed me at the morning service. English Methodism, insofar as it was represented at Kingsway Hall, is considerably more "High Church" than Methodism in America. The accent was upon liturgy, with the repeated chanting of canticles and psalms. I am accustomed to the barest minimum in an audible pastoral prayer, America being noted for "quantitative colossalism" in lesser things than intercession. I think we spent ten minutes in formal prayer at Kingsway Hall, yet the time passed quickly, for it was divided by choral responses into six lesser periods, each devoted to a special theme—thanksgiving, prayer for the nation, for the Church, for the sick (remembered by name), confession of sin, and personal silent intercession. It did seem, I confess, that English Methodism had taken seriously Christ's words: "My Father's House shall be called the House of Prayer for all nations." God was clearly at the center of things in a living way; He was not a mere "Trade Name." I was impressed also by Dr. Soper's personal leadership, by his excellent voice in the singing, but even more by the quality, and brevity, of his sermon. In America sermons tend to make up in length for what they lack in depth. The sermon at Kingsway Hall was scarcely longer than the prayer, yet every minute was wisely utilized. The idea was simple enough, and presented with directness and color. Illustrated from the story of Job, and from the life of Christ, a human being was not required to know all the answers; he was, however, required to trust and obey, and in trust and obedience he was, by Divine Grace, unconquerable. Surely, I felt, this was a relevant message for England in her hour of trial.

A little before 3:00 P. M. I accompanied Dr. Soper to his stand, near Marble Arch, in Hyde Park, where, on a later trip, I was privileged to hold forth, and cordially invited to return. On every side were street orators hard at work, each with a meager handful of amused listeners. One gesticulating prophet endeavored to substitute fury for clarity. Not far away a Roman priest read from a manuscript to an indifferent flock. When Soper climbed into his "Kingsway Hall" pulpit, a wooden platform with a simple lectern, the crowd rallied around him at once; two hundred people, possibly more, were all attention. They had learned to expect him, and a real entertainment, every Sunday at three, as similar crowds expected him on Wednesdays at Tower Hill.

I am not certain that John Wesley would have approved the enormous time Dr. Soper consumed in an undistinguished political free-for-all. Understandably, there was no formal program, merely the impromptu give and take of questions, answers, insults, and laughter. Whatever John Wesley would have thought of the performance, for he introduced Christ to the English masses by street preaching, it was, I confess, "a good show," as Dr. Soper intended it to be. There was, of course, no continuity of topic, simply the hit or miss of attack and counter-attack. Yet the hour and a half yielded two or three things particularly memorable. Most important, I think, was the fact that Soper gave himself utterly to the people, that he met them exactly where they were, on the level of their own manifest interest, that he accepted, and occasionally returned, their rough sarcasm, in no sense setting himself above them. I do not know on what level John Wesley began his street-corner discourses, though I am fairly certain that he began on the level of religion; in any case the people understood him and flocked to hear him. As Woodrow Wilson has written of Wesley's preaching, "It was no pastime to hear him." If Donald Soper seemed to be giving his veteran Hyde Park controversialists a stone rather than bread, it is possible that the appearance was misleading, for at the close of the wordy contest he declared that he represented the Church of Christ, without Whom modern leaders, in their attempts to solve human problems, were the blind leading the blind. During the years of Dr. Soper's weekly self-surrender to the people of Hyde Park, many thoughtful listeners, for the most part silent auditors to the noisy prophets of the right and the noisier critics of the left, had followed him from the Marble Arch hurly-burly to Holy Communion at Kingsway Hall. In any case, he was selfless enough to be vigorously at work in the vineyard of the Lord, while his carping critics, remaining timidly behind the doors of their empty Churches, had often been talkers rather than heroes. Whatever comparison with John Wesley might yield, Donald Soper was building a living bridge to the masses; if at one end of the bridge was a babble of words, at the other was the Son of God.

It would not be accurate to say that no coherent idea emerged from the Hyde Park interplay. Dr. Soper repeatedly asserted that he was a Pacifist and a Socialist, that Russian Communism was Socialism's worst enemy, that all political platforms, whether of the left or of the right, were powerless aids to human well-being unless the moral energy of true religion evoked responsibility among the people. One fanatic accused Soper of living in the lap of luxury; Soper replied that the accuser was merely "a sillier ass than usual, if that were possible." Another excited brother, bald-headed and cross-eyed, declared his ecstasy that the Church had been weakened by the war. With pontifical finality and choleric bombast, he delivered the motheaten pronouncement that the Church was unadulterated hypocrisy. He referred continually to the War of 14-18, by which he meant 1914-1918, but his dubious reference evoked gales of laughter. I had the feeling that, while the noisy participants in the wordy battle were mainly extremists of one kind or another, the great majority of silent listeners were Soper's actual interest. From these thoughtful citizens recruits had been secured for permanent Christian consecration.

Later, as we discussed the value of the Hyde Park enterprise, Donald Soper asserted his opinion that a different mentality existed in Wesley's time. The people were then prepared to hear sermons on the street. Today's pagan mentality could be reached only by a pagan bridge. There would be, I believe, some disagreement on this point among men qualified to speak. Did not St. Paul speak continuously of Christ to Roman pagans? Yet the hour and a half of "public yelling" (Soper's own characterization) amid storms of abuse, on a crowded Sabbath, done with prayerful consecration to the glory of God, was clearly redemptive in purpose. If but one soul thus returns to the House of Prayer, is there not rejoicing in Heaven?

In the evening, following the formal interview, I accompanied a Kingsway Hall Gospel Team as it went forth in fear and trembling to conduct service near the entrance to the Underground's

Holbourne Station. Five young people, from sixteen to twenty-five years of age, took their turns upon a platform. Each spoke briefly to the theme, "What Christ Means To Me", while the others constituted the nucleus of a congregation. One older youth, clearly frightened at his task, remained at his post like a good soldier. Consulting his notes, he delivered an original and penetrating analysis of the meaning of total Christian living in the modern world. I thought to myself: "Whatever has given this frightened young man the courage to stand up on a London street and confess his faith in Christ is surely one with the faith of St. Peter, St. Paul, and the martyrs." The leader of the group, a handsome youth with curly hair and ruddy complexion, explained that Christ had put joy and light into the daily monotony of his toil as a hospital porter. Furthermore, as a member of the Labor Party, he was convinced that only the Spirit of Christ could make England's Socialist Government the Servant rather than the Tyrant of the people.

Donald Soper expressed the belief, in our interview, that English Methodism had been largely untouched by Kierkegaard, Barth, and Brunner of the present, as well as by Thomas Aquinas and John Calvin of the past. He feared that the majority of English Methodist pastors were thinking solely, and superficially, in "Come to Jesus" terms. An intellectual revival was greatly needed. Dr. Soper's own influence had been James Ward. One of Ward's disciples had been his Cambridge tutor. He acknowledged himself "High Anglican" in his thinking, emphasizing Holy Communion as the historic confession of Christian discipleship, but accenting as well a heightened personal relationship with God and a broadened social application of Christian Ideas. He was not Unitarian in theology, he asserted, but would enquire of Trinitarians what they meant by the Incarnation. His own belief stressed a dynamic rather than a static Incarnation. In the morning sermon he had declared that there were many things Jesus did not know, but as a Hero of absolute obedience and trust He had shown men how to live; thus He had won His central place in human affection. Beyond this pragmatic statement, Dr. Soper did not discuss his Christology.

He regarded G. K. Chesterton, whom he had known, as "a very good Christian, but a very bad Roman", an embarrassment rather than a blessing to the papal flock. Rome's unity was apparent but not real. Upon investigation, the living faith of the few was overshadowed by the paganism, and by the multiform divisions, of the many. Rome's political hierarchies, he said, had everywhere distinguished themselves as despotic, reactionary, and parasitic. Non-Roman Catholicism, he added, could do Christ's work more efficiently separated from Rome, than burdened with Rome's dead weight.

Methodism, as a particular Branch of Protestant Christianity, had but one reason for existence, said Dr. Soper, the same reason it had had from its beginning with the Wesleys — to build a bridge from Christ to the people. When Methodism ceased to be evangelistic, as Wesley had been, it ceased to be Methodism and surrendered its reason for separate existence from the Church of England. Methodism had been historically a bridge from Anglican formalism to the formless masses. It had to continue so to be, or find its abandoned task taken over by "lunatic fringe" cults, full of enthusiasm but without the redeeming grace of knowledge.

Donald Soper, at my request, described briefly his Order of Christian Witness, which he characterized as "the Christian Commando Movement *plus*." Under his direction, for example, between two and three hundred ordained and lay preachers, young and old, had descended for one week upon the city of Plymouth. Soper pictured himself an absolute authoritarian, as Wesley and Booth had been before him. A military organization functioned more effectively. Under his supervision, an assistant was the actual Commanding Officer. There were five captains over sub-groups of sixty, and in each sub-group ten teams with appointed leaders. Each team of six conducted forty to sixty brief services during the week's campaign — in saloons, restaurants, factories, on the streets, in the parks, wherever a handful of people could be gathered. A series of short talks emphasized what Christ meant to the speakers, in relation to the total of contemporary life, and concluded with an invitation to Holy Communion on the following Sabbath. Several hundred men had received Communion, in common confession of Christian dis-

131

cipleship, at the appointed hour. An organization to carry forward the good beginning had been left behind. Three hundred ordained and lay preachers went on similar mission to Hutter's Field, each man paying his own way. All lived frugally at a common commissary, and slept camp style, on the floor, in a warehouse. One thought of Francis of Assisi's five thousand Poor Friars gathered for common counsel at Michaelmas, or of Wyclif's Lollards, Loyola's Jesuits, or Wesley's laymen. England has an established tradition of serious Christian bridge-building to the people. Perhaps this tradition has had something to do with the fact that the war and postwar rationing of necessities, which, after all, rested squarely upon the honor of individuals, worked with conspicuous success in England. At any rate, it was a hardheaded Presbyterian, Woodrow Wilson, as we have said, who observed that the Wesleyan revival had saved England from the madness of the French Revolution.

Donald O. Soper not only carried forward concrete projects of Christian Evangelism throughout England, he was also administrator of half a dozen social service projects in London, directly within the orbit of the West London Mission — hostels for men, hostels for women, places of refuge for drunkards, houses of rehabilitation for prostitutes, homes for orphaned children, medical aid centers. Efficient workers, each with a sense of Divine Call, made possible these specialized services. Some of the finest staff members had been converted from the London streets. In all, an annual budget of 25,000 pounds was involved. Surely this was alert Christianity, not shrunk into a memory but alive to the present and the future — for where authentic Christianity is, there is also live compassion toward spiritual and material need. Christ took upon Himself the human tragedy, and, in Toynbee's terms, "transfigured it." He was, so to speak, the Future, and is still the Future, pressing in with healing upon the Present.

NEWTON FLEW

My desire to interview Newton Flew, Principal of Wesley House, British Methodism's Cambridge graduate school for ministers, was due in part to repeated statements by mutual friends that he was one of England's major Christian voices, but even more to my belief that American Methodism could profit immeasurably from renewed contact with her English original. It has been said, perhaps unjustly, that, culturally speaking, America is one part England and two parts water. There were times in England when I felt this accusation to be true. If the English people are to be explained, as I believe they can be, by five things — the weather (adaptability), tea (mildness), cricket (patience), walled gardens (domestic stability), and the Church of England (theological coherence and morality) — the last of the five, both on her own account and through her cluster of lusty Non-conformist offspring, has given a degree of continuity to British Christianity apparently lacking in America. Americans would naturally rebel against the exchange of the Bishop of Rome for the King of England as Supreme Governor of the Church, yet the thirty-nine articles of the Church of England, maintained against heretical assault partly by imperial might, are, I think, a sort of written Constitution for Ecumenical Christianity. I read them again carefully between services at Christ Church Cathedral, Oxford, and was impressed with their simplicity and relevance. In all sincerity I believe that this non-Roman Christian Constitution has made a greater contribution to ideological unity and balance throughout the British Free Churches than they would, perhaps, be prepared to acknowledge. For the same reason I am convinced that American Methodism stands only to gain by constant contact with Mother England, as Antaeus gained strength from Mother Earth.

Newton Flew had been continually praised in my hearing as a particularly excellent representative of English Methodism, combining skill as an administrator with profound intellectual penetration, genuine scholarship, and power as a preacher. He had then retired from his post as President of the Methodist Conference in the United Kingdom, and was in direct touch with the work.

We came at once to an analysis of modern influences in British Methodism. Mr. Flew acknowledged that Niebuhr, Barth, and Brunner had a considerable following among the younger men. In his opinion, however, "The skirts of salvation were always disappearing around the next corner" in Niebuhr's writing and preaching, and Barth and Brunner, though Swiss, merely represented one wing of the German theology that was always going to extremes. Man, and the manhood of Jesus, almost disappeared in Neo-Orthodoxy. It might be concluded, he said, from reading Niebuhr, Barth and Brunner that Matthew, Mark, and Luke had not been written, that Christ was indeed Divine enough to save men but not human enough to understand them. The older Methodist theologians had maintained a better balance between the Deity and Humanity of Our Lord, a truer basis for faith and conduct, and a deeper reinforcement of the human spirit by the Spirit of God. No doubt the work of Barth and Brunner had been a valuable corrective to the relativistic trend in modern theology, Mr. Flew asserted, but the cure in some respects had proven worse than the disease, for, in all honesty, the Deity of Christ had seldom been wholly surrendered even by humanizers like Harnack. If we had to give up either Luke or Paul, and fortunately we were not confronted with such a choice, Christendom might better profit, for a time, from the surrender of Paul than of Luke.

It was not to be understood that the older British Methodism, in its refusal to go along with the newer Barthianism, had been in any sense Unitarian. Quite the contrary. Methodism from the beginning had maintained a clear Trinitarian witness in England, whether or not in America. Every statement of faith compiled by British Methodists, in recent as well as former times, had vigorously proclaimed the resurrection of the Divine Image in man solely through the merits of Christ Crucified and Risen. Christ was indeed the Divine Self-Revelation to man, the Will of God made flesh.

Mr. Flew deplored the fact that the war had laid heavy demands upon the time and energy of all British theologians. The writing of treatises had been left of necessity to American thinkers. His own time had been consumed in unavoidable administrative responsibilities. Hodgson and Taylor had produced thoughtful work, but in the main wartime England had been forced to sacrifice theological productivity.

British Methodists were possibly not doing the thorough reading one should expect. The Americans, Edwin Lewis and Lynn Harold Hough, however, were widely read. No Thomist influence was strong enough to be worthy of note, and, except among Barthians, little attention was given to Kierkegaard or Pascal. The French Existentialists, religious or non-religious, were all but unknown in England. In a word, English Methodism was English, and far more deeply dependent upon its own great tradition than upon any imported influence. John Wesley's faith and thought were still powerfully felt.

Mr. Flew had been a member of the original group which had defined the purpose, and established the pattern, of the World Council of Churches. He had championed its cause from the beginning, recognizing the great service it could render as a rallying center, in theology and in fellowship, for all non-Roman Christians. As a matter of fact, Methodism itself from first to last had been an essentially Ecumenical Enterprise, emphasizing the Lordship of Christ and genuineness of discipleship rather than creedal difference; it had therefore been naturally adapted for its role in the World Council. Obedient faith in Christ as God and Saviour, the definitive emphasis of the World Council, had provided Protestantism with the central Christian standard, a unifying principle in a time of relativism. At an earlier period there had been some British Methodist feeling against participation in the World Council of Churches, but denominational provinciality had completely given way to the Ecumenical mind. At many recent Conferences of United Kingdom Methodists, there had been virtually unanimous approval, for example, of Methodist union with the United Church of South India. Protestantism's tendency toward endless branching and sub-branching had apparently run its course; the defining spirit of the present was one of unity. Yet this did not mean the end of Methodism, nor indeed the end of any legitimate Branch of the Tree of Life; rather it meant that each denomination had to perfect its usefulness as an instrument of Christ in the light of the common standard. Mr. Flew felt that English Methodism, numbering nearly a million members, and deeply committed to God, was a compact and dependable instrument in the Lord's hands.

There was feeling neither of need nor of desire for reunion with Rome. Mr. Flew had always quoted to his opening classes in Systematic Theology Rome's own statistics, that there were then 390 million non-Roman Christians in the modern world — in Greek Orthodox and Protestant Churches alone — and but 330 million Romans. A clear minority among confessed Christians could hardly expect to be taken seriously in its familiar assertion that it possessed a monopoly on Truth.

British Methodists would be found in all major political groups, but in strongest numbers in the Liberal Party. The Liberals would, in all likelihood, vote with the Conservatives on current issues. Mr. Flew's son, then 24 years of age, had written an admirable article on the thesis that no real reason existed why a young Englishman could not at one and the same time be a Christian in religion and a Conservative in politics. Conservatism offered the only hope for a preservation of individual dignity against bureaucratic encroachment; it offered also the only practical, as against Socialism's doctrinaire, mobilization of community resources for the solution of community problems.

On the international scene, Mr. Flew believed, from reports sent to him in confidence, that, even now, Germany was more to be feared than Russia. She seemed to be possessed, in her post-war disintegration and defeat, with a mad lust to regain her military might for one purpose only — to bring all Europe to her own present despair. This was not post-war day-dreaming, but the actual meaning of information issuing from the German interior. Christian responsibility clearly demanded the feeding of the fallen enemy, sharing the few crusts the enemy had not destroyed. However, Germany had, of her own accord, to become, and might indeed develop, a contribution rather than a curse to the Free World.

English Methodism had been particularly concerned with Evangelism and its problems. Complete support had been given to the

Christian Commando enterprise and to various home visitation campaigns. Similar efforts, like the Order of Christian Witness directed by the individualist, Donald O. Soper, had attracted some attention, but Methodism had never been excited about fads in Evangelism. Steady and long-term evangelistic thinking and preaching had rather been her Sources of power. One excellent device for the recovery of central Christianity in the American Church was Methodism's own Ecumenical movement. England's vigorous emphasis upon central Christianity, said Mr. Flew, would thus wholesomely counter American theological diversity.

I myself have seen the value of old-world/new-world contact among American representatives to the Oslo World Youth Conference. On our journey from the States, I witnessed young Americans clearly under the impression that they were going as missionaries, as bearers of enlightenment, to darkened Europe, yet prayer, the reading of Christian classics, and meditation on the total meaning of the Faith, normal symptoms of authentic zeal, were not accented. After Oslo, I noted, among similar young Americans, returning home, a marked difference. Prayer-meetings and Bible classes had reappeared, with considerable prominence, on the ship's daily orientation program. One cannot but conclude that young America did not so much minister at Oslo, as she was ministered to, in the deeper things of the Spirit.

There are those in America who will not find the idea acceptable, but I have been continually impressed that American Christianity has as much to receive as to give in fellowship with Britain and the Continent, both in clarity of central Christian Conviction and in true Ecumenicity. Perhaps what American Christianity has most to offer in return, in addition to bread for the hungry, is her recognized ability to invent new procedures, and her well-known tendency to turn Ideas into Deeds.

Do we not indeed owe to England, Mother if not Father of Protestantism, Industrialism, and Democracy, not only the seeds of our best culture, but, remembering the Island Fortress at first standing alone in World War II against Nazi aggression, an important measure of our Freedom?

An Irish American, to whom I expressed these convictions, became apoplectic, and proceeded to list England's known sins — failure to pay war debts, theft of her original Empire, etc. "John Bull is a Devil," he said, with gestures. But is it not the American way to give even the Devil his due? No one, so far as I know, has accused Uncle Sam of an excess of sinlessness.

THE GERMAN METHODIST POINT OF VIEW

T. W. E. SOMMER

We are familiar with our opinion of the German people; we are less familiar with their post-war opinion of themselves and us. There perhaps exists no uniform viewpoint, but the most striking interpretation I have heard I received at the American Army Headquarters, Frankfurt, Germany, from the head of German Methodism, Bishop T. W. E. Sommer, an M. A. from Cambridge, a gray-haired, kindly man of vast learning, great administrative ability, and considerable personal charm. He proved an excellent interpreter of the postwar German mentality, and an articulate apologist for German history. One of three Methodist bishops in Europe, his area then covered the whole of Germany, with 320 pastors and 1100 deaconesses. A second Episcopal area was Scandinavia, a third southern and eastern Europe.

Bishop Sommer described, at my request, his own background. Following graduate study in England, he had been for many years a missionary in Asia Minor. For two decades he had been associated with Frankfurt's Prediger Seminar, as teacher, dean and principal. In the office of bishop he had succeeded Otto Melle.

German Methodism, he said, had remained close, in theology and procedure, to English Wesleyanism, first to penetrate Germany. The first German Methodist pastor had been, interestingly enough, a converted Jew, Jacoby. American Methodism had entered Germany at a later date. At the present time all branches of German Methodism are united. An active influence among German pastors stemmed from Barth and Brunner in Switzerland, but mainly German Methodist thought had been guided by German theologians. I asked if German rationalism, or higher criticism, had been strong in Methodism. On the contrary, Bishop

Sommer replied; the denomination had offered faithfully the Christian alternative to rationalism. I explained that American Methodism, theologically speaking, had been described as under-nourished. Bishop Sommer replied, smiling, that German Methodism had gained new vitality during and following the War. The denomination, deeply committed to Christ as one with man and one with God, was strong and growing, possessed a clear idea of its faith and its work, was without apology or hesitation in pursuing its task. Its Deaconess work, in hospitals, homes, and churches, was stronger than similar work anywhere in the world.

I asked if Deaconesses, unlike Roman Nuns, were permitted to marry. No rule restricted them from marriage, the Bishop replied. In the main the group was composed of young women with a deep sense of Divine Call. Dedicated to selfless Christian service, they received no salary, though a pittance for incidentals was provided. Later in the day I visited the Deaconess "Mother House," one of Frankfurt's finest hospitals. I smiled upon diminutive Germans in bassinets, who still spoke the international language. A Kodachrome I did not secure, a scene which will remain forever upon my heart, included a dozen Deaconesses laboring side by side with German workmen in the rubble of their former hospital, completely destroyed by Allied bombs despite a large Red Cross clearly visible on its roof. These angels of mercy, singing and laughing as they worked, were removing usable bricks from the debris of their once proud edifice overlooking the river Main. I was reminded of a paragraph in an essay by my student, Franz Brand, describing Roman Nuns as they removed corpses from bombed English dwellings. A by-stander had remarked, "I wouldn't do that for a million dollars." "Neither would we," a bride of Christ had instantly replied. Not for money were these German frauleins doing the work of men, with songs instead of sighs.

What was to be the future of racial discrimination in Germany? I asked. Bishop Sommer answered: "What Europeans and Americans do not understand is this: Hitler was the most un-German man who ever lived in Germany. If you listed all the things that Germans are not, he would have been the epitome of them all.

The day the Frankfurt synagogues were burned at Hitler's order, I talked with Germans and with Nazis throughout the city; not one approved. Americans unfortunately cannot think of Germany before 1933; other Europeans remember only 1914 or 1870. Hitler and his maniacs did not represent our longer history in any slightest degree. A recent book by a Jew, on the sufferings of his race, explicitly stated that Germany has been, historically and on the whole, the kindest nation in the world to Israel. Also, in view of her total history, Germany has been the most peaceful nation in Europe, as any statistical study will show."

These statements, I confessed, surprised me. I replied: "The average American would respond to your remarks with the question: 'How shall Hitler's acceptance by the German people be explained?'" Bishop Sommer asserted forthwith: "Hitler was a product of German despair. If the Allies had given the pre-Hitlerite German government half the concessions they gave Hitler, he would never have come to power. High American tariffs, during the Republican 20's, made German economic recovery impossible. At no time did a majority of Germans approve of Hitler. He came into power by a deal which declared communist votes illegal; he thus received a small plurality. At the height of his success, say in 1943, in a free election eighty percent of the German people would have voted against him. Those who did vote for him at the beginning did so only with the idea: 'In our plight, what can we lose by the experiment? If we do not like him, we can always throw him out and elect a new government.' Later they discovered that Hitler's police stranglehold on Germany made his removal impossible. Elections were at no time free. Those who voted for him discovered their mistake too late, but in any case their votes constituted only a frantic experiment in the face of economic despair. If Germany is given an opportunity to recover her characteristic life, at the opposite extreme from Hitlerism, she will prove herself the friend of Europe. If the Allied idea is not to destroy Germany, her economic life will have to be given a chance, under suitable safeguards, to the end that she may assist in the formation of a United States of Europe. It is falsely believed that Germany has vast

141

natural resources. She has, in fact, less natural resources than any major power; she has truly wrought miracles with her slender store. Given a chance, Germany will strengthen all Europe and prove a blessing to mankind. The Marshall Plan greatly benefitted Europe, including Germany, so long as it was, as its statements declared, not an expansion device for American big business, but an effort to put European industry on its feet."

Bishop Sommer mentioned that Americans and Germans were alike in their acceptance of hard work as a dignified and essential part of life, a mentality, he said, not shared by other Europeans. Again and again American G-I's, to him and to innumerable other leaders, had said they felt much more at home with the German people than with other Europeans, recognizing a common pattern in home life and social behaviour. The G-I's felt themselves objects of suspicion in England and France, they had said.

Whatever the complete truth may be, I knew, as I left Bishop Sommer, that I had been in the presence of a first-rate Christian mind.

During the afternoon the Bishop placed his car, a small French Renault, with a young chauffeur, at my disposal. We toured bomb-pocked Frankfurt, once one of Europe's most beautiful cities. A third or more of Frankfurt was rubble, but industrious Germans had already made great strides toward recovery. A typical congregation, whose church had been totally destroyed, had cleared away the debris with their own hands, and renovated a basement room for worship. I was shown the magnificent "Brown House," once occupied by the Nazi leaders who had murdered its Jewish owner. Information that the edifice was a Nazi resort had been sent by Germans to Allied airmen; the house had been precision bombed early in the war. At another point Nazis had burned a Jewish synagogue, and, in its place, erected a bomb-proof shelter of concrete and steel. Every block had its piles of rubble where houses or hotels or stores or factories had once stood. Homes seemed to have been singled out as bomb-targets. A few downtown hotels, the Palmengarten, and a huge office-building had been carefully exempt from air attack. Everywhere I was impressed with German thrift and industry. In contrast to England, where backyards are flower gardens and lawns, every square inch in Frankfurt was occupied with growing food-stuffs. If hard work and self-reliance deserve a reward, Germany deserves better than Kremlin dictatorship — and the East-West drama in Berlin is now but in the Second Act.

THE ENGLISH UNITARIAN POINT OF VIEW

L. P. JACKS

It would not be true to say that there are no alternatives to Christianity in the world, for many do exist, in fancy and in fact. For myself, an American species of Christian, I am quite convinced that there are no equal or superior alternatives, should Christianity be judged solely by its fruits, among which, according to Toynbee and Dawson, is our beloved Free World Civilization. Indeed, as we were told by Señor S. de Madariaga, in our class in Twentieth Century European Civilization at Oxford University, "When Europe forgets its inheritance of intellectual freedom from Socrates, and its greater inheritance of spiritual autonomy from Christ, it will cease to be Europe."

The alternatives to Christianity are manifold in form, though few in distinction of content. Unitarianism, itself a Christian product, which has made a vigorous and in part necessary, though unsuccessful, bid to humanize traditional Christianity, is historically distinguished by a single affirmation, its belief in Christ, as He called Himself, the Son of Man, that God is not a Trinity but a Unity. At any rate, in humanist development, it often seems a competitor, one of the alternatives, to Christianity, and, as such, deserves respectful examination. I was keen, therefore, to interview the former Principal of Manchester College, Oxford's Unitarian School, L. P. Jacks, well known in America as lecturer in forty-eight States, and as editor of the HIBBERT JOURNAL (which, under another respected Editor, published, not long ago, my essay on the distinguished Liberal American, James Luther Adams). It seemed to me that one way to rediscover Christianity was to talk to an articulate individual who believed in Jesus' heroic humanity, and who, in rejecting in part traditional Christianity, might know exactly what he had rejected.

144

I do not wish to imply that L. P. Jacks, benevolent octogenarian, was a typical Unitarian. As a matter of fact, as he explained to me at his beautiful home, Far Outlook on Shotover Hill (overlooking Oxford as Oxford overlooks the rest of the world), he had spent his entire administration at Manchester resisting a concerted effort to turn the then undenominational College into a Unitarian School. As he put it, "I resolved that they would make Manchester a Unitarian College only over my dead body." As long as he had remained, his resistance to sectarian encroachment had succeeded. At his retirement, the deed had been done.

I wondered for a moment if I had been misinformed. My host appeared a Trinitarian in revolt against the Unitarian development in the traditional Christian Family. On this point he soon set me right. He had been zealous to keep Manchester open to students from all denominations, to resist its becoming a closed Unitarian corporation. In his own thinking he was definitely a non-Trinitarian, and therefore, he supposed, a Unitarian, though he did not call himself one, and rather resented the term, for he felt that his own religion had life in it, and he was quite sure, he said, that Unitarianism did not. Unitarianism, in his view, was the collected absence of any particular viewpoint worth mentioning; it was an intellectual fog, and clearly had no future whatever. He considered William Ellery Channing, he said, a classical Arian in his thinking, of no present importance; contemporary Unitarian leaders, he added, were equally sterile.

L. P. Jacks was by no means a representative Unitarian, though I would like to think of him as one, since he was so vigorous a Theist. He had no sympathy whatever with atheistic or merely humanistic Unitarianism, primarily, he felt, an American departure from Christianity. I described my Unitarian friend and fellow-clergyman in an eastern American city, who openly acknowledged his atheism and sought to change the word "Church" on the front of his congregational hall to "Society." "But for God," declared Mr. Jacks, "there could be no atheists." The atheist received, he said, his voice and his intellect from God's goodness. The moment God withdrew His hand, he added, the atheist would die forever. The atheist, it seemed, was trying to light the Sun by striking the match in his hand.

Mr. Jacks was emphatic about the Divine Self-Conscious Existence and the Divine Goodness. He considered the Old Testament God one-sided, a Deity interested only in righteousness. God was interested in everything and everybody; He gave and maintained life in all. Man's very ability to disobey God—to lie and steal and kill—was a Divine Gift, though the sinner thereby misused his good freedom. Disobedience to the Divine Will and non-cooperation with the Divine Purpose were real choices of Unreality; they constituted the serious part of the human problem—politically, socially, personally. It was God who maintained life even in the disobedient.

Mr. Jacks said that he did not often pray. When he did, his prayers centered in thanksgiving. He thanked God for everything. The Good Lord had uniformly treated him better than he had deserved. (My father, a Syracuse University varsity guard, and a Fundamentalist Methodist minister, used to say, often, the same thing.) He asserted that God was not the Author of Wickedness as well as of Good. On the contrary, God was the Author only of Good, as Christianity had always taught; moral evil issued from man's misuse of the Divine endowment.

This was a Christian view of God and Man. Wherein lay Mr. Jacks' departure from the Faith? In his Christology, he asserted. He did not regard the New Testament as history. The books of the New Testament were Cult Documents, produced by the messianic preoccupation of the time. Jesus Himself had been of no transcendent importance. Galilee had been full of enthusiasts of one kind or another. There had been at least six messiahs in Christ's own generation, stirring up revolt against Rome, urging men to prepare for the Kingdom of God which would soon, and did, destroy the Empire of the Caesars. The Roman authorities at Jerusalem had been instructed to catch these trouble-makers and put them to death. When Jesus had ventured into Jerusalem, He had promptly been caught and killed. The disciples, full of enthusiasm and excitement, had mistaken their own wishful thinking, and a few reported dreams, for Jesus' bodily resurrection.

Peter and Paul had made this Fable the basis of their preaching. If men would believe in Christ's resurrection, they would share His triumph over death. The Gospels of Matthew, Mark, Luke, and John, though perhaps begun in the middle of the First Century, were, as we had them, very late products, certainly as late as 150 A. D. The Epistles and the Revelation were early expressions compounded of wild messianism and the resurrection Myth. The so-called Christian Gospel was an invention of Peter and Paul and the writer of the Revelation; the unknown authors of Matthew, Mark, Luke, and John simply had believed what Peter and Paul had created from pious illusion, and had adorned the facts to fit the Fable. The Gospels undoubtedly had been written by members of the Christian Cult who had known nothing whatever about Jesus' actual life.

"Christianity then, in your estimation," I enquired, "has no existence in fact, but is entirely the creation of fancy?" "Exactly," Mr. Jacks replied. "And would you acknowledge," I asked, "that this non-Christian interpretation, or guess, about Jesus is by no means the only possible reading of the same set of historic facts?" "Of course," said he. "I have merely outlined my own guess, a conjecture shared by contemporary French New Testament criticism. Christianity, constructed upon the reverse interpretation of the same history, needs no apology."

Trinitarianism, he went on to say, was the best reasoned system of theology, nobler than Hebrew Monotheism, and certainly more intellectually respectable than Unitarianism. However, God could not be the End of an argument; He was rather the Beginning of all arguments. Reasoned theologies could describe God only in part. He overflowed all the definitions, and was not concerned about the Name by which He was called. He was close to every man, in every man, in every nation, in every religion. When a man worshipped, the whole man, greater than the sum of his faculties, was instinctively and immediately conscious of God, the matter-mind Unity of the Infinite Universe, the Source of man in His image. Mr. Jacks denied that his position was Pantheistic, though he acknowledged that it was closer to Pantheism than to Christianity. I mentioned a resemblance to Kierkegaard in the idea that God was known by direct experience, not by rationalistic argument. Berdiaeff also, I pointed out, had emphasized that theology was always a postscript to God's direct encounter with men. The transcendent, and immanent, glory of God could not be encompassed by deistic, atheistic, or even theistic, rationalism. Yet was it not Christian theism which had defined God as beyond definition?

I wondered if a strain of Pacifism lay behind Mr. Jacks' view that God was equally present in all men. "Was it right to resist Hitler?" I enquired. "Certainly," he replied. "We were forced to choose between two evils. Crushing Hitler was the lesser wrong; it would have been a far greater wrong to have allowed him and his cutthroats to go unchecked."

"And what about Russia?" I asked. "That's a difficult question," he answered. Russia, he said, was afraid of the atomic bomb then held only by Great Britain and America. There was talk of war between the United States and Russia, but as yet there seemed no sufficient reason. It was not possible to ascertain whether the Russian motives involved aggression, or protection, against Europe. In any case Russia's single-party dictatorship had no sympathy for democratic procedure. The Russian autocracy knew only how to give orders. In addition, Russia's underhanded infiltration methods in Eastern Europe had demonstrated her untrustworthiness.

In any event, the only possible policy toward Russia, on the part of England and the United States, was undeviating firmness. "Stalin's kind must understand that we will stand no nonsense from them." If on this basis war became inevitable, the war would be of Russian choosing. In all likelihood, however, firmness would guarantee peace, since Russia needed time to treat her wounds, had well in mind the atomic bomb, was then transporting German scientists behind the Iron Curtain to develop it.

I explained, in closing our interview, that I was anxious to have Mr. Jacks' suggestions about necessary steps if Christianity were to reassert its healing ministry in the world. His answer proved a startling challenge to all who, justly or unjustly, call themselves Christians. Just one thing was necessary, he said, and repeated his assertion again and again: Christians had to believe in Christ's Deity, in His resurrection from the dead, and declare in Him the Hope of immortality — personal, conscious immortality, not the survival of influence which meant personal extinction. He believed in personal immortality for all who were worthy of it, he said. Some, however, who believed in God did not believe in personal survival. Nevertheless, Christianity, and the Hope of personal triumph over the grave, were inescapably united. The preaching of a certain Hope of resurrection in Christ had given Christianity its First Century power. Peter and Paul had taught that Christ had risen from the dead, not in myth, nor in symbol but in visible reality, that all who believed and lived in Him would assuredly share His victory over death. In this Faith the martyrs had gone singing to their torture in Rome's Coliseum. Death had meant nothing to them. Even Christianity's victory over sin was secondary to its victory over death. The believer directly shared Christ's Superhuman defeat of the Grim Reaper, and left his sins, together with death, in the tomb. Exactly this victory of good over evil, of life over death, had been and remained the specific Christian message. If this message were not true, as Paul had said, there was no Christianity. "If Christ be not risen from the dead, then is our preaching vain, and your faith is also vain." If Christianity recovered this, its historic Gospel, and proclaimed it with assurance, asserted Mr. Jacks, it would conquer the world.

THE CZECH COMMUNIST POINT OF VIEW

HANUS LOMSKY

We are familiar with Communism from our point of view. We are perhaps less familiar with Communism in its own eyes. A Czech Jew, convinced to the marrow of the truth of Communism, shall speak for himself.

My appointment was for ten A.M. at Prague's Communist Headquarters. I had been warned to guard my speech from the moment I entered the building, for the elevator porters would certainly have been informed of my visit.

There had been some miscarriage of efficiency, however, for, though the appointment had been made by an official in my hearing, no one at headquarters knew anything about it. Bedrick Geminder, assigned to interview me in the absence of Rudolph Slansky (then General Secretary of the Communist Party and therefore the Kremlin-approved master of Czechoslovakia), had not come down to his office. Geminder might come in at eleven o'clock. Finally, a young woman appeared, speaking very little English, and, at my request, phoned to confirm that the appointment had been made. Within a few minutes I was ushered into a private office and presented to Hanus Lomsky, deputy of Geminder and Slansky. He apologized profusely for the inconvenience I had experienced, and for the failure of a Communist official to keep an appointment. He mentioned that confusion was not uncommon at headquarters, that some lack of smoothness was inevitable in the new government.

Lomsky was a most gracious individual, and I confess I liked him immensely. Handsome, intelligent, and with his British English, he reminded me strongly of a youthful Oxford Don. He had lived in England during the War, he said, at a distance from Hitler's anti-Semitic mania. During the same period Geminder and Slansky, also

150

Jews, had lived in Moscow, whence they had returned to direct Czech Communism.

By way of starting the interview I explained that sympathy existed in America for the Czech people, since America widely believed in economic brotherhood, and could not but approve legitimate or freedom-preserving measures to translate the idea into reality. However, I continued, Americans were widely out of sympathy with one-party dictatorships. Lomsky smiled, and replied: "Yes, of course. I understand the Western two-party system, though I do not believe in it."

With this introduction I proceeded to my first topic: "Being a professor of religion in an American college and an ordained minister, I am interested in your own religious background." Lomsky had not, I think, expected this kind of question, but received it courteously. "I am a Jew. I was raised in an extremely religious Jewish home. My parents, who died here during the German occupation, were devout members of an Orthodox synagogue. I am an atheist. I do not know the religious backgrounds of Geminder or Slansky."

"Is there an essential connection, in your opinion," I asked, "between Communism and Atheism?" At once Lomsky replied: "In the original Marxist materialism there was, of course, a necessary atheism. However, in Communism as it now exists in the Soviet Union and in Czechoslovakia, there is no necessary link. On the contrary, it is recognized that there is much common ground with religion. Historical Christianity, of course, was preoccupied with otherworldliness; it is therefore irreconcilable with Communist this-worldliness."

"But," I replied, "in the Sermon on the Mount, with its Golden Rule, 'As you would that men should do unto you, do ye even so to them' there has always been a clear thisworldly demand."

"Yes," said Lomsky. "I myself believe that Christ did teach economic as well as spiritual brotherhood, but His followers have not always understood Him."

"Also," I added, "as you know, many persons, who are not materialists, have acknowledged a profound influence from Marx — Nicholas Berdiaeff, for example, a leader in the revolt against the

Czar, a member of the Kerensky Government, and one of the great Christian thinkers." I outlined briefly my interview with Berdiaeff in southern France.

"Yes," said Lomsky. "There have been many such men. My father, with whom I used to discuss my political and economic philosophy, never approved of my atheism. In fact, he heartily disapproved of it. But he did agree with me on economics."

"Pursuing the theme of religion," I continued, "is the new government program, to pay all clergymen's salaries, designed to strengthen or weaken religion?" I acknowledged that the question might be unanswerable. It was widely believed, I explained, that state support of the clergy meant an inevitable decrease in spiritual vitality. For example, in a Sudetenland city, evacuated by the Germans, a church building was now used, at different hours, by two Czech state Churches and one free Church. The Czechoslovak National Church claimed three thousand members in the city, but had from six to nine persons at its worship. The Czech Brethren or Presbyterian Church claimed nine hundred members, but had fifteen at its service. The Methodist Church had sixty members in the area, but received eighty each Sunday for song and sermon. Would state payment of clergy salaries have a similar effect throughout Czechoslovakia, and was this effect the purpose of the measure?

"Not at all," said Lomsky. "The purpose is a very simple one. We wish to make clergymen officials of the state, in order to secure their help in promoting the well-being of the community as a whole. You see, Communist morality means that the community must take precedence over the individual, though the individual is important also. In time of harvest, for example, when city dwellers must help gather the crops lest they be destroyed, we want the pastors to urge their congregations to participate. Wherever there is a community need, we want the clergy to rally their people to help."

"Christianity, of course," said I, "regards the community as of great importance, but views the individual soul as of eternal worth to God; other aspects of personality than economic and thisworldly ones must therefore be taken into account."

152

"To Communism also," said Lomsky, "the individual is important for more than economic reasons. After all, what is the community but the individuals who compose it? It is really for the individual's total well-being, not only his material advantage, that our regime exists."

"Would any change be made," I enquired, "in the present teaching of religion in the public schools?" "None," said Lomsky. I pointed out, smiling, that it might be of interest to him that considerably more religion, indeed considerably more Christianity, was publicly taught in Communist Czechoslovakian schools than in Capitalist American schools. Two hours a week, with serious assignments for credit, were offered through the student's sixteenth year. As the Czech Minister of Information had put it: "We do not want our children to learn about Caesar and not about Jesus Christ." Lomsky, an atheist, was deeply amused that religious education was illegal in American public schools.

"Has there been," I asked, "any special conflict between the new government and the Czech Churches?" "Only with the Roman Church," Lomsky replied. "You mean," I asked, "because of its Ecumenical character centered not in Prague but in Rome?" "No," he answered. "Rather because the Roman Church never protested against the German atrocities here, apparently approving German anti-Semitism, yet the same Church widely criticizes the Communist program. And yet," he said, smiling, "the statement often heard is partly true — 'In Czechoslovakia all our Communists are Catholics' — for, after all, seven out of ten Czechs are Catholics, at least in name."

My next question moved to a different theme: "Is the purpose of the new regime to establish an independent Czech State, or to make Czechoslovakia a Russian province?" "There is no other purpose," Lomsky replied, "than to make Czechoslovakia entirely independent, a true nation on its own account, yet ideologically one with the Soviet Union."

"What three things," I asked, "would you list as the major accomplishments to date of the new government?" "That is easy to do," replied Lomsky. "First of all I would mention international

153

security. Munich will not happen again. We have given Czechoslovakia standing among the nations; it need no longer depend on the self-interested whims of England and France, of a Chamberlain or a Herriot. We have at last secured, for Czechoslovakia, independence from outside forces. We cannot again be treated like step-children by Western powers willing to sacrifice us to save their own skins.

"Our second achievement is freedom from want. We have destroyed inflation. We have abolished unemployment; we have given all workers a sense of ownership in their industries, a real security in their jobs. They are no longer dependent upon the whims of proprietors, nor robbed to make capitalists rich. They neither have to beg for work nor bow and scrape like slaves before capitalist masters. They know at last that they are the masters, that no one can take their jobs away from them, that they need not fear unemployment. Every man in Czechoslovakia can have a work-permit and enjoy his share in the profits formerly accumulated for unproductive owners."

"What has happened to business concerns that have not shown a profit under Communist management?" I asked. He replied: "If of value to the people, they have been subsidized. If not, they have been renovated or liquidated, as under private management." The system seemed to be, in fact, not Communism, but State Capitalism.

"Does not unemployment exist in a new form?" I asked. "That is, what of the former owner of a factory, whose business was nationalized since he had more than fifty employees, who is not acceptable to the workers' committee now in charge? Can he secure a work permit?" "Yes, certainly," said Lomsky. "The difficulty has often been that former owners could *do* nothing. They had never worked usefully, and in the new regime no place could be found for them. If they work at all, it has to be at some menial task for which skill is not required. There have never been more than eight thousand such persons in the whole Republic, and that number is now diminished since many have found something to do. A few have been too proud to apply for work permits, preferring to lean on friends, or even to starve."

"Has there not been some discrimination," I asked, "against

workers, peasants, or former owners, who voted the white ballot (against the Communist regime) in the last election?" "None whatsoever," asserted Lomsky. "The leader, Zapototsky, recently stated in a public address that no discrimination existed, or would exist, against non-Communists. All workers, whether Communists or not, are entitled to receive work cards, and to share in the benefits of the new regime. And, in many cases, former owners, who were skilful managers, are now employed as operators or directors in their own industries."

"Do these directors receive larger salaries than average workers?" "Of course," said Lomsky. "Much larger."

I remembered a Czech Christian factory-owner, whose story had been related to me by a Prague pastor. He had enlarged his business in twenty years from one to six hundred employees. Under the new government he had been promptly dismissed as manager of his own business. But the Communists in control had reckoned without psychology: production had forthwith dropped to an all-time low. At the workers' own insistence the man who had built the business had been brought back as its manager — at five thousand crowns a month ($100 white, $25 black), while a Communist overseer received seven thousand five hundred ($150 white, $37.50 black). There seemed little point in relating this tale to Lomsky.

One advantage of the system, said Lomsky, had been the unique solution of the housing shortage. The law is simple: there must be no more rooms in a private flat or home than there are members in the family — six members, six rooms; two members, two rooms — not including hallways, kitchen, and bath. Extra rooms have to be rented out at government-controlled price.

The Communist leader continued his summary of government achievements: "One must not overlook the greater dignity and self-respect, the increased social privileges, our regime has given individual workers. For the first time, the former lower classes enjoy vacations and holidays in the country. Our one-party government exists only for the worker. A fascist regime is a one-party government existing solely for the aristocracy. That is why we call our regime 'The People's Democracy'."

155

"Our American New Deal," I suggested, "could be correctly understood only as a similar attempt to secure the economic brotherhood of man *under a two-party system,* where freedom from political coercion, as well as from illegal seizure and arrest, was guaranteed by the Constitution and the Bill of Rights."

Lomsky at once replied: "Greater freedom exists here than in the United States. For example, what public law has protected Negroes from lynching in the South? Communists are fired daily from their jobs, in or out of the government, in your country; European Communists cannot secure visas for entry into America. You are an American and therefore presumably a defender of Capitalism. Did you have any trouble securing a visa for entrance into Czechoslovakia?"

"None," I admitted.

"You see," said Lomsky, "we are not afraid of difference of opinion. We know that the vast majority of our people approve our People's Democracy. We know that they will always vote for the government which is their servant."

"But," said I, "in our country a Henry Wallace may start a Third Party; a Second Party may compete for the highest offices. Here in Czechoslovakia, if I am rightly informed, only persons approved by the Communist Party may run for office."

"It is true that we are a one-party government," said Lomsky. "However, you must understand that before our regime began there were, at one time, thirty Parties here, many set up merely to confuse and mislead the workers. Complete chaos reigned. If Democracy means that the will of the people shall prevail, the Party the people have selected must assume the total responsibility of government. And even now, a non-Communist who secures one thousand names on a petition can run openly for any office in the Republic." (I had a mental picture, possibly incorrect, of what would happen to the thousand persons who dared thus to oppose the Party in power.)

"Do you mean," I emphasized, "that the non-Communist who openly campaigned for the highest office in the land would not quietly disappear into Siberia?"

"Exactly," said Lomsky, smiling. "Of course, we are in a state of transition, and no one knows the future. But as far as I know, this freedom remains intact."

"There is a slight difference of opinion, is there not," I enquired, "about freedom of the press?" Said Lomsky: "In your country freedom of the press means protection for fascist ideology, protection for misinformation, distortion, and war-mongering; it means freedom to print what is not true and what is not moral." While waiting in the outer office, a copy of the magazine, CZECHOSLO-VAKIAN LIFE, had been handed me. In the main the issue was devoted to the six hundredth anniversary of the founding of Charles University in Prague, to which the world's Universities had been asked to send representatives. The invitation had been given the cold shoulder by some Western institutions, notably Oxford. Space was also given to Czech industry, finance, national resources, and wholesale trade. I was specially interested, however, in an article by Dr. Oscar Kosta, head of the foreign press department of the Ministry of Information, entitled *Where Freedom of Information Really Exists*. Kosta, reporting the Conference on Freedom of Information called by the Social and Economic Council of the United Nations, in which representatives of fifty-four countries had participated, accused Western delegates of satisfaction with an abstract idea of freedom designed to protect war-mongering, fascist ideology, and racial and religious discrimination. To quote:

The contrast is quite clear. The Slav delegates and with them the delegates of Albania, Hungary and Rumania, did not want a mere abstract conception of "freedom of information" which on the basis of this abstract formulation would leave all doors open to damaging influences which have already been rooted out by the People's Democracies and which must be mercilessly annihilated wherever they still appear.

It was clear from the article that Communist freedom of information meant freedom *from* criticism and freedom *for* support of the regime in power, suppression of "damaging influences" or embarrassing facts, to be "rooted out" and "mercilessly annihilated."

"And what of Czech crops and commodities," I asked, "that are widely believed to be moving quietly but steadily either into Russia or into the Russian zone of Germany?"

"Look here," said Lomsky, using a characteristic British expression, "that is mostly falsehood. It is true that our distribution of the recent cherry harvest was terribly inefficient. People went out directly to the farmers and bought the cherries, so that very few reached the stores, but that was simply due to our faulty system of distribution. None, so far as I know, went either to Russia or to Germany. Some potatoes have been shipped into the Russian zone of Germany, and occasionally we have received raw materials from Russia and from other nations in exchange for half of the manufactured products."

"Simply our American Good Neighbor policy?" I asked. "Exactly that," said Lomsky.

Hanus Lomsky had been frank and patient for an hour and a half. Whatever the objective truth may be, and it lies perhaps in the wide divergence between Communism in theory and totalitarianism in practice, Lomsky was clearly a devoted supporter of the new Czech experiment. Again he apologized that a Communist official had failed to keep an appointment, that I had been inconvenienced. He shook my hand warmly at my departure. "Will there be War?" I whispered at the door. He smiled, and answered firmly, "We can say with absolute certainty that there will be no War."

THE CZECH PROTESTANT POINT OF VIEW

JOSEPH L. HROMADKA

The people of the Churches, said my Prague friend, were out of sympathy with Joseph L. Hromadka, then Dean of the John Hus Theological Faculty, who had said that he was not a Communist, but had defended Communist policy and practice against every attack. I explained that I planned the same day to journey to Senohraby, Hromadka's summer home, to see him, that his essays and my own had been published side by side in Princeton's THEOLOGY TODAY, that I had used his volume, *Doom and Resurrection,* in college classes. Hromadka was an excellent person, corrected my informant courteously; all who knew him liked him.

Arrived in Senohraby, it was soon disclosed that Hromadka and his family had departed for Geneva and Amsterdam. However, my journey was not in vain; I drank tea with Dr. and Mrs. Lukl, Hromadka's parents-in-law, and with Mrs. Lukl's sister and her husband. All spoke English, and together they answered, in part at least, many questions I would have asked Hromadka. Mrs. Lukl, a great lady indeed, was a most generous hostess, and her husband was particularly helpful in clarifying his son-in-law's attitudes.

I had read Hromadka's accounts of the new Czech regime. There had been, he had argued, a complete breakdown of liberal leadership, not alone in Europe, but particularly in Czechoslovakia. He did not share the materialistic philosophy of Communism, nor did he believe in a one-party government, yet he did believe in the economic brotherhood of man. To quote him directly:

> The path of my faith and the path of the communistic activity intersect one another, but they are not identical; they are of an essentially different nature. . . . My present position was

prepared by a long study of T. G. Masaryk's profound analysis of the moral, spiritual, and social decay of what we call the modern man and the liberal capitalistic society. . . . My theology — based on the Biblical testimony of the real presence of the Crucified and Risen in the deepest depth of human misery, and of His ultimate victory at the end of times — has assisted me in my theological effort to keep my faith free from any self-identification with our social or cultural order, free also from the Western civilization which I greatly cherish and love. . . . The Christian witness has got to be carried on where there is no security. . . . The most dynamic historical forces and the witness of the Church meet and intersect one another. . . . The Church of Christ must not keep herself behind the Maginot line of defense. She has to carry on her witness and struggle precisely on the spot of the greatest danger.

He had advocated "creative readjustment to the social process" in order to direct it toward the will of God. The new Czechoslovakian regime was composed of two elements, though the West saw only one of them: 1) Russian expansion, and 2) Czech bourgeoisie breakdown. Before the February Revolution the desire had been to make Czechoslovakia "a meeting place where the best and the most creative elements of the East and the West would come together and construct a common ground of cooperation." Since February, 1948, Czechoslovakia, by Roosevelt's promise to Stalin at Yalta, to gain his aid in defeating Hitler, had been entirely enclosed within the Eastern orbit. Two groups of Czech Christians existed: those who sought to withdraw from contact with the regime in power, and, on the other hand, those who desired to make their Christian witness where policies were formed. Hromadka's position in itself was clear enough, but the question sprang to mind: "How does all this differ from the policy of Laval, Petain, and Quisling?" I asked aloud. "What precisely is included in the phrase, 'the Breakdown of Western Liberalism'?"

Dr. Lukl, senior elder in his Prague Presbyterian congregation, pointed out, with a smile, that he was neither a theologian nor a philosopher but a man of medicine. It seemed to me, I said, that three ideas were possibly implied, with only partial truth, in the word "breakdown": on the economic level, a failure of capitalistic society to share with peasants and workers the nation's goods; on the theological level, a failure of vital faith in either Protestant or Roman Christianity; and third, a failure of true creativity in literature. Dr. Lukl believed, he said, that these ideas were basic in Hromadka's view.

It occurs to me that a fourth failure is possibly included, nominally rather than actually, in Hromadka's mind — a failure of the democratic process itself. It may be, in part, Hromadka's view that only a one-party government possesses sufficient power to carry through needed reforms, to curb anarchic freedom. Social benefits, he may believe, can not be achieved in a two-party system where one uncreative leadership rapidly succeeds another. Should this approximate the Hromadka philosophy, is it not a basic departure indeed from Western political thought? Is it not, as a matter of fact, identical with the philosophy expressed so vigorously in *Mein Kampf* — contempt for the common man's alleged ability to distinguish right from wrong, to select wise men to rule him rather than fools? The political philosophy of Lenin, Stalin, and their successors, though it shouts to the skies its exclusive purpose to share the good life with the masses, clearly possesses a similar distrust of the average man's moral sagacity. Someone must do his thinking for him. It is diffcult to believe that Hromadka has overlooked this Great Divide in political, and theological, thought. Dr. Lukl did not feel qualified to speak on this theme for his son-in-law.

Dr. Lukl stressed that Hromadka was a Communist neither in membership nor in philosophy; he rather held the view that, to help the people, you had to remain on speaking terms with the leaders in power. Because of his friends in the West, particularly in America and England, Hromadka was valued by the new regime, and granted unusual liberties — including foreign travel.

Hromadka had not agreed with every policy of the new regime. He had been, in fact, the government's severest critic; he had reserved the right to speak freely against any specific program. At a recent election, he had been asked by the Communists on three occasions to urge the people through the newspaper to vote for the Communist candidates and to ignore the white ballot, the only alternative. Each time he had refused; the people, he had said, should decide for themselves.

Every popular criticism of the new Czech government, Dr. Lukl asserted, could be said with equal truth of American government. It was not safe to oppose the Communist regime in Czechoslovakia, I observed. It was not safe to oppose the Capitalist regime in America, Dr. Lukl countered. Hromadka, he said, was tolerated in Czechoslovakia, exactly as Wallace was tolerated in the United States. Was there not a difference, I asked, since Wallace's Third Party had been constitutionally protected in America, but no similar second or third party would be protected by Law in Czechoslovakia? The good doctor made no reply.

The Lukls vigorously denonunced the German occupation. Senohraby's beautiful resort hotels had become German youth hostels. Roving young Germans had destroyed property at the Hromadka villa, and had been very angry when reprimanded. The beautiful villa grounds were in poor repair; workmen had not been available for many months. When American day laborers had moved *en masse* to Detroit defense plants, I pointed out, American house and ground keepers had been equally scarce. I was impressed that the Czech and the American New Deal had been, in small part, similar, except that in America the Republican alternative had been maintained by law and long custom. Political freedom, as a matter of fact, does seem to stand or fall with vigorous two-party competition. Political machines, in a two-party system, can deliver many votes, perhaps enough to win closely contested elections, but they cannot deliver all the votes. You can't fool all the people all the time. Even with entrenched and powerful labor and political machines swaying elections, American independent voters have frequently upset all calculations, for robust alternate regimes were always available.

Dr. Lukl stated calmly: "You in America will have the same kind of government we have in a few years." I replied: "We had it first, in a measure, in the New Deal, and may thus have been immunized against it. Anyway, we like our kind of government. We like freedom." "What is freedom?" asked Dr. Lukl. I replied: "Freedom means: no coercion in matters of conscience — an authentic alternative to the regime in power."...

The square in front of the Amsterdam Reformed Cathedral was jammed, after the service as before, by a milling, expecting throng, dimly aware that some strange New Day was dawning. A dozen mounted and motorcycle police sought in vain to maintain order. I paused a moment to greet Emil Brunner, in whose home at Zurich I had enjoyed so rich a fellowship. I exchanged brief greetings with my friend, Ralph W. Sockman, and my then Bishop, G. Bromley Oxnam. Presently Joseph L. Hromadka and his lovely daughter, Nadia, met me for our appointed interview. We made our way through the multitude to a nearby street cafe, where, over coffee, we discussed at length the meaning of modern Czechoslovakia and the World Assembly.

I described, at Hromadka's request, the overall conclusions of my interviews in his native land, and the gracious hospitality accorded me at his summer home in Senohraby. I then explained a central theme I wished him to discuss. He had mentioned in his article, *Between Yesterday and Tomorrow,* in Princeton's THEOLOGY TODAY, the breakdown of bourgeoisie leadership in Czechoslovakia, which, in his opinion, had necessitated the present regime. What, precisely, was to be included in the phrase, "the breakdown of bourgeoisie leadership"?

He had not primarily referred, he said, to the failure of the Benes Government to provide employment nor to the essential relativism of liberal European theology, though both economic failure and theological confusion had existed in fact. He had rather meant simply the failure of bourgeoisie statesmanship to offer a coherent program. Only feeble negative criticisms of Communism's integrated program had been offered. No clear affirmative plan had appeared. A complete loss of bourgeoisie political and economic creativity had been painfully evident. Jan Masaryk had said to him, "No articulate alternative to the Communist program seems in evidence. There is no strong leadership." The Communist regime, asserted Hromadka, had come into existence as an endeavor to fill the vacuum created by feeble and uncertain bourgeoisie leadership, which had lived only in the past, in dreams, and had been manifestly unable to grasp the problems of the present. The Communists had had a clear idea of where they were going; they had had a definite program to offer; their political victory had been inevitable. With no liberal alternative in view, the people had simply chosen, or, more accurately, had accepted, the present regime.

I was reminded at once of Gabrielle Marcel and his principle of creativity. Totalitarian bureaucracy, he had asserted, could come into power only when spiritual and economic creativity, in a context of freedom, had been lost.

Hromadka had explained to the Communists, he said, his agreement with their endeavor to establish the economic brotherhood of man, but also his fundamental disagreement with them on three issues. He did not share their view that no power, no authority, no judgment existed outside the historical process, for he believed in the God Self-Revealed in Jesus Christ. He did not share their view of human nature, that man was merely a unit in the group, for he believed in man's individual transcendent reality as an object of Divine Love. Finally, he did not believe, should the Communist objectives be fully realized, that a virtual paradise would result, for both original sin and man's thirst for God would continue to exist.

I mentioned that there is wide agreement with the desire to establish economic brotherhood, provided it is brotherhood as fellowship, rather than brotherhood as loss of freedom. However, while any Christian must disagree with Communist philosophy on the issues Hromadka had outlined, permanent disagreement must also exist on still another issue — the Communist one-party dictatorship and its police state, which had robbed the people of all actual liberty, while at the same time preserving the forms, the name, and the façade of freedom.

Hromadka regarded the Czechoslovakian regime in quite another light. It was clear, as he talked, that his arguments were identical in every particular with those of Hanus Lomsky. I felt, as Hromadka spoke, that he saw the Communist regime only as it sees itself, in the ideal. I am certain that his contact with the regime, as a member of its Central Action Committee, as one who has been admitted to inner Moscow circles, is based less on actual than on theoretical approval; that he has not himself experienced loss of freedom nor the rough edge of totalitarianism universally experienced by the common people. He did not believe, he said, that there was any loss of freedom in the new Czechoslovakia. He did not agree that the new government was a one-party dictatorship.

I began to list for his information specific events, reported to me by peasants, factory workers, coal miners, merchants, intellectual and religious leaders — incontrovertible evidence that an actual slavery had been quietly substituted under a nominal freedom by the new government: a Czech Brethren pastor, in Kladno, the Czech Pittsburgh, forced for two months to labor in a forest for offering criticism of the regime in his pulpit — a man in this congregation who had gone to work one morning as usual, whose wife had been visited by a Communist Committe three hours later, with the information, never enlarged, "You are at liberty to marry again any time you wish; until then, we will continue to pay you in part, your husband's salary." Hromadka grew visibly agitated at these findings, and asserted that he had been unaware of them. As a member of the Central Action Committee, he demanded to know in detail every violation of freedom, that he might register vigorous protests in the Central Committee itself. He could not believe that five men, in one parish, in recent months, had disappeared without trial, that no one had dared demand a government explanation. If these miscarriages of justice had actually occurred, he said, he had no sympathy with spineless local citizens who had permitted them to happen without protest. He considered this spinelessness an evidence of the bourgeoisie breakdown he had described.

I pointed out that common citizens, not enjoying Hromadka's position of influence in the government, were convinced not alone that protests would do no good, but that they themselves would be the next to disappear without trial. I mentioned that every leader I had interviewed had asked me not to mention his name. If freedom actually existed, these leaders would not have felt it necessary to remain anonymous. I lengthened the list of events exhibiting fear and slavery. Hromadka's excitement increased visibly at each item.

It was apparent that he is, for the present, able to see the Communist regime only in the light of its theoretical purposes, that he is inwardly unable to perceive or accept the actual disappearance of freedom, self-respect, and personal dignity (except in government offices, or the shelter of private hearts and homes) in his native land.

I cited the fact that in America two or three Parties could actively compete for election, that a Wallace could bid for votes, that no similar alternatives could be offered in present-day Czechoslovakia. I quoted Dr. Lukl, Hromadka's father-in-law, who had said to me at Senohraby: "Hromadka is the Czechoslovakian Wallace, the open critic of present policies." Nadia said to her father, at this point: "Grand-father ought to have a higher opinion of you than that."

I mentioned, as he was no doubt aware, that the Czech people looked upon him as a Quisling, a Laval, a Collaborationist. He knew he was so regarded, he said, but had had to choose one of two courses of action, either to withdraw in cowardice from a realistic attempt to grapple with the new regime in the interests of justice, seeking to make the Christian witness where policies were made, or to enter bravely into the government itself, without consideration of personal risk, to seek to make reason and the will of God prevail. I suggested that the time might come when he would be forced against his conscience to go along with the regime in power, or to make a complete break at risk of personal martyrdom. In the land of John Hus, I added, he, Hromadka, could also conceivably become a martyr for freedom. This, he replied, was not an issue for him to consider, one way or the other. The event would be in the hands of God. In the meantime, he could but continue his endeavor, not to withdraw in cowardice, but to witness with courage for justice in the new regime's Central Action Committee.

THE CZECH ROMAN POINT OF VIEW

JOSEPH BERAN

I was privileged to accompany fifteen American Methodist pastors, led by Karl Quimby, on their scheduled visit to the Czech Roman leader. A bumpy ride in a crowded special bus brought us, not too rapidly, through abundant Czech harvests, to the fifteenth century castle where Archbishop Beran awaited us.

Before the Archbishop's elevation, as a popular anti-Nazi, he had been imprisoned two years in a German camp. The Roman seventy percent of the Czech population have long considered Beran their most beloved priest. I am privileged, I believe, to mention him by name, though I do so with fear and trembling, for the interview was neither exclusive nor in secret, and his views are already known. His courageous stand against Czech tyranny has filled, since then, our headlines.

We were received by the Archbishop's gifted secretary-interpreter, and led at once through the castle's lofty halls and spacious chambers into an audience room. The Archbishop, who has repeatedly demonstrated his sympathy with non-Roman Christians, received us warmly. He was rugged of countenance, kindly, with a short, stocky figure dressed in scarlet. Again and again through the interview he lifted and replaced a tiny skull cap, reminiscent of a similar high Anglican gesture performed at the name of Jesus, or, if you will pardon humor at the expense of a great man, reminiscent also of the cap-removing gesture of an organ-grinder's monkey. No one could have treated us with greater respect; no one could have answered our questions with greater magnanimity.

Dr. Quimby, leader of the American delegation, described the mutual love of Roman and non-Roman Christians; he then raised the question of religious freedom under the new regime. The Archbishop explained that no hindrance existed to the public celebration of the Mass; restrictions, however, had been imposed upon preaching. Criticism of the Communist Government was not tolerated. Many Roman priests had been imprisoned for pulpit remarks. It was true that the Roman Church was supported by the State. Free-will offerings would not have sufficed, said the Archbishop. State support of all pastors was apparently soon to be given. Church attendance, high during the Nazi occupation, and low in the interim of freedom, had risen again as the people had experienced the heavy hand of new oppression.

Was it possible, I asked, for a Roman in theology to be a Communist in economics? This was not even a possibility, asserted the Archbishop. A few Roman Church members, particularly in industrial areas where non-Communists lost their jobs, were "paper" Communists. With this factor in mind, Roman policy had been to leave politics to private conscience. Occasional factory workers were both Communists and Romans, but they were seldom Communists for other reasons than expediency. However, some economic principles, advocated by Communism, had been advocated earlier, he said, by papal encyclicals. Romanism did not approve the methods of a revolutionary police state; likewise Romanism disapproved the materialism to which Communist principles had been attached. The issue was Christ or Caesar, God or Mammon, and Romanism was committed unequivocally to Christ.

What relationship existed between Romanism and the Czechoslovak National Church? I asked. Did a modernist movement still exist? Had the National Church been formed primarily around Unitarianism or primarily around Czech nationalism? Entirely around rationalism in theology, asserted the Archbishop. The Czech national spirit had played a very small role in the creation of the new Church. No possibility of fellowship existed between Romanism and Unitarianism. Atheistic Communism had been an open enemy of Roman Christianity, but Unitarianism had proven the friend who betrayed, who silently undermined Christian foundations. There was no Roman modernist movement at the present time.

Were Jacques Maritain, Etienne Gilson, and Christopher Dawson read by Czech Romans? I enquired. Very much so, answered the Archbishop; both he and his secretary visibly brightened at the names. I had been privileged, I explained, to interview these Roman writers.

Another American visitor asked: "Does the Czech Roman Church have parochial schools?" The word "parochial" had to be explained; we then learned, since Czechoslovakia had long been strongly Roman, that church schools had not been necessary, for both pupils and teachers in public schools had been Christian. In Slovakia, where church schools had been conducted, many, if not all, had been closed by the Communists.

What of the attitude of the Roman Church toward the World Council of Churches? I asked. The Archbishop explained that Romanism had recognized value in all Ecumenical movements, but had not been permitted by papal action to participate in them. Movements toward unity, especially those centered in Christ as God and Saviour, were all to the good.

I stated: "It has been said that the Methodist Church in Czechoslovakia lives by converting Roman Christians; what comment can be made on this theme?" The Methodist Superintendent had hastily interpolated that Methodism had grown primarily among persons "lost from Rome." After quiet meditation, the Archbishop said: "The Roman religion is difficult and complicated; its intricate life has developed through the centuries. It is not an easy religion, and some of our people are looking for a lighter and simpler form of Christianity." I was pleased that the Archbishop had been so frank, and perhaps not wholly inaccurate, in his remarks. I thought also: "Peter said the same thing at the Jerusalem Conference recorded in the Acts of the Apostles. Israel's religion had become an intolerable burden; Christianity offered the Grace of God on simple, universal terms to all men." The Archbishop's statement was therefore accurate, and, at the same time, a tribute and a rebuke to both Communions. Romanism has a simple theology, centered in Christ as "very God and very man," but has developed complications in ritual and administration. Methodism is fast developing a complex

169

administrative system, but to some extent seems watered down in theology. John Wesley, who possessed a thorough theology, stressed spiritual experience. Methodism today, its critics vigorously though inaccurately declare, stresses a reduced spirituality in a context of theological confusion. Thorough theology, however, can no longer be taken for granted. Conspicuous neither for theological clarity nor spiritual vitality, contemporary Methodism, it seems possible, is in danger of becoming machinery with a diminished destination, a juggernaut traveling at great speed in an uncertain direction. A great part of Protestantism seems, in part, in similar plight. The Great Reformers levelled an identical charge against Romanism in the fifteenth and sixteenth centuries. The hearing of a Divine Summons to true renewal is, it appears, always overdue. Indeed, the great need of the West is a new Reformation, a Renaissance of clear theology and vital spirituality; perhaps, for this reason, the New Delhi World Council of Churches, has been publicly called "'The Second Reformation." The contemporary world battle, it seems, is between Christ and Caesar, but among nominal supporters of Christianity a second battle rages, it appears, between Christ and lesser christs. The purge of Anti-Christ must precede, parallel, or follow the victory of Christ over Caesar, of God over Mammon. The forces of Anti-Christ are always a fifth column for Caesar, as in Hitler's France collaboration obstructed resistance. France was liberated, neither by collaborationists nor by German generosity, but by spirited resistance from within and armed Allied invasion from without. The kingdoms of this world, it is fervently hoped, will be reclaimed from Caesar in a better, United Nations way.

At the close of the interview, in response to a visitor's appeal, the Archbishop offered prayer, asking that the Divine Blessing accompany us on our way.

THE GREEK ORTHODOX POINT OF VIEW

BISHOP PANTHELEMON

At the Amsterdam Assembly Western Protestantism seemed to receive more than its fair share of attention, for the Greek Orthodox Church alone numbers two hundred million members. My anxiety to find a true representative of Greek Christianity was well rewarded. I met Bishop Panthelemon, of Edessa in Greece, the fifth day of the Conference. From childhood, said the Bishop, he had desired to train for the priesthood. His long beard and black clerical robes were not of the West, yet his flawless English overcame the apparent strangeness. A high point in his Christian growth, he said, had been his two and a half years at the Episcopal Seminary in Philadelphia. From earliest memory Christ had been a daily Reality to him; the unequivocal Christology of the World Council had enabled his Communion to join. The Greek Orthodox Church is guided by its Council of Bishops, each with a single vote. In early centuries the Bishop of Rome, as the first Bishop of Christendom, said Panthelemon, had had one vote, had been regarded as first among equals. Rome had gone her separate way into papal absolutism, but the Greek Church had continued as in Apostolic Times, exactly as described in the Fifteenth Chapter of the Acts of the Apostles. The Bishop of Constantinople, said my friend, is first in rank in Greek Orthodoxy, the Bishop of Jerusalem second, of Antioch third, of Moscow fourth, etc. The Moscow patriarchate, under its distinct political regime, has developed elements of its own, yet remains, he said, within the family of Greek Orthodoxy.

An effort would be put forward at the Assembly, I pointed out, to change the World Council from a loose confederacy, a mere conference table, into an organic union. Bishop Panthelemon explained that Greek Orthodoxy would continue to favor a loose confederacy, a free and equal association of distinct Communions.

Organic union would mean an official leadership, presuming to speak for all, and the over-riding of significant differences. Domination by Western Protestantism, with its confusion of tongues, he said, was feared as a possible departure from classical Christianity, as a substitution of external uniformity for the unity of the Holy Spirit.

An attempt would also be made, I reminded my friend, to eliminate present differences in clerical ordination and in the administration of the Holy Communion. Bishop Panthelemon believed it a mistake to overlook or over-ride different basic interpretations of the Sacrament. The Greek Church accepted Christ's words simply: "This is My body," though it did not use the Western term "transubstantiation." In the Holy Communion the participant received the Holy Spirit; if without faith, he received damnation. Greek Orthodoxy could share no common Sacrament with Protestant denominations which considered the Holy Communion merely a memorial of ancient events. The Greek Church, the Bishop asserted, had not drifted into the Scholasticism of the West. Essentials had been continuously emphasized, and nonessentials neglected. Western rationalism had not developed in the East.

Of the Assembly's conflict on economics, Bishop Panthelemon spoke with conviction: "Communism is misunderstood in the West when it is regarded simply as a system of economics which a Christian may take or leave. Communism, from beginning to end, is a total system of life and thought in basic and irreconcilable opposition to Christianity's Free World. Communism is exclusively the system of Anti-Christ, and can be understood accurately only in this light. No communion of any kind, on any level, may exist between Communism and Christianity. Communism is not against religion; it is only, and forever, against Christianity. "Hromadka," he said, "has not as yet perceived the true nature of Communism. It is obvious, also, that Hromadka would not have been permitted to attend the Assembly had Moscow not known in advance what he would say and that he would champion the Russian cause. Greece has experienced the Communist assault on Christianity much longer than Czechoslovakia; the real issue, not yet clear to

Hromadka, and no longer in doubt in Greece, is Christ or Anti-Christ."

I left Bishop Panthelemon with a profound sense of spiritual benediction, of deep unity with Greek Orthodoxy, one parent, or grandparent, of all Christian Communions. I was grateful for the Bishop's gracious invitation to attend, if possible, the Greek Orthodox celebration of the nineteen hundredth anniversary of St. Paul's crossing from Troas to Philippi, the entry of Christianity into Europe. One cannot forget the words of the Apostle to the Gentiles, who later wrote to the Christians of Philippi and the world:

Let this mind be in you, which was also in Christ Jesus;

Who, being in the form of God, thought it not robbery to be equal with God;

But made himself of no reputation, and took upon him the form of a servant, and was made in the likeness of men;

And being found in fashion as a man, he humbled himself, and became obedient unto death, even the death of the Cross.

Wherefore God also hath highly exalted him, and given him a name which is above every name;

That at the name of Jesus every knee should bow, of things in heaven, and things in earth, and things under the earth;

And that every tongue should confess that Jesus Christ is Lord, to the glory of God the Father.

For we wrestle not against flesh and blood, but against principalities, against powers, against the rulers of the darkness of this world, against spiritual wickedness in high places.

Wherefore take unto you the whole armour of God. . . .

173

THE AMERICAN POINT OF VIEW

HENRY J. CADBURY

No one can deny the tremendous influence exerted in England, America, and beyond, by our Friends, the Quakers. They may have ceased to quake individually, but they are responsible for a considerable quaking in the minds and consciences of contemporary men. They are a standing criticism of our age of violence and egoism, much as St. Francis of Assisi, with his wooing of Our Lady Poverty, was a breathing rebuke in his age to the twin lusts of power and money sometimes then characteristic of Pope and Emperor alike.

An Atlantic crossing provides many entertainments, to be sure, but none equal, I think, to the opportunity for getting acquainted with personalities and the modern groups they epitomize. To prepare myself for the appointed interview with Henry J. Cadbury, Quaker, then Chairman of the American Friends' Service Committee, and Professor of New Testament at Harvard Divinity School, I first attended a morning hour of silent meditation on D-Deck in the company of a dozen Friends. The only interruption to the hour of complete silence, which I found immensely useful for catching up on my own private devotions, was an excellent short discourse by a handsome youth on the idea that the meaning of Christianity was responsibility, developed inwardly but expressed in social action.

The Glory of the Undefined

Mr. Cadbury made it quite clear to me that the defining thing about the Quaker is his refusal to define his faith — not that he does not have a faith, but rather that it is at once too im-

174

mense and too personal for objective simplification. "Quakers are quite as able to depart from the absence of an objective Creed," he said, "as other Protestant groups from the presence of one." An objectively stated Creed does not, of itself, seem to penetrate into the thinking of the rank and file, even of those who profess belief in it. Since much of religion, particularly of Christianity, is personal, and, as Kierkegaard pointed out, cannot help but be, the Quaker is on reasonably good ground in placing his whole emphasis on this element, and neglecting objective creeds altogether.

There is a very real danger among the Quakers, Mr. Cadbury acknowledged, of falling into one or the other of the twin heresies of relativism and solipsism. But, as I suggested, this danger seems equally to challenge the whole of modern Protestantism, with or without hierarchical organization and creedal objectivity. In other words, Quakerism and all the rest of contemporary Protestantism seem a good deal alike — both in nature, in the presence of inner divisions, in their problems, and in the common battle against Secularism.

It did seem clear, as we talked, that Secularism was definable even if Quaker Christianity was not, for Secularism was simply our old acquaintance — Materialism, or, in the terminology of Sorokin, also of Harvard, and our common friend, Sensatism, the simple belief that sensory reality is alone real. Quaker Christianity was thus defined at least negatively: it was opposed to Secularism. By the same token it was also thus defined somewhat positively: it was in favour of a universal recognition of the accompanying reality of the spiritual — a supersensory reality considered as a relationship with God.

Two things seem clear in an affirmative definition of the structure of Quaker belief — the supreme importance of immediacy in a living relationship with God, what the early Quakers called "The Inner Light," a Divine influence in every soul in no way to be identified with the socially-conditioned conscience, and second, a strong sense of social responsibility, conditioning conscience itself with the Absolute in relation to the Relative.

A further affirmative idea in the body of Quaker thought emerged in our discussion from a glance at history. In 1828 Elias Hicks, a Long Island farmer, led a revolt from Orthodox Quakerism primarily over the controversy raging at the same time in other Protestant Communions, particularly in New England Congregationalism, as a cleavage between Unitarians and Trinitarians. Today the Hicksite Quakers number about fifteen thousand in America, as over against approximately eighty-five thousand Orthodox Quakers. As in Congregationalism itself, however, the passage of a hundred years has modified or shattered the significance of the original division, for an occasional Hicksite Quaker turns out to be a marked Evangelical, believing in the Deity of Christ and the sinfulness of man, and more than a few Orthodox Quakers indicate their equally marked leaning toward Unitarianism. Even an occasional Fundamentalist puts in his appearance in both groups.

Thus Trinitarianism, in one form or another, turns out to be the dominant theology, expressed or unexpressed, of the contemporary Quaker mind, not the less vigorous and not the less influential in forming all other beliefs because seldom set down in cold type. And Trinitarianism is the correct word, for, upon examination, the Quaker idea of "The Inner Light" which lighteth every man coming into the world, by its divorce from man's socially-conditioned conscience, is clearly identifiable only with the classical Christian idea of the Holy Spirit — the immediate Presence of God in every human soul, particularly influential in the soul of the believer for the obvious reason that any influence is stronger and clearer where it is accepted and obeyed.

This spiritual quality in Quakerism has been emphasized even at the very heart of its activity for social reform, for Quakers were often Socialists in England where Socialism was a strongly religious movement, but are seldom or never Socialists on the European Continent or in America where Socialism and Secularism are often identical. The great word to the Quaker in the field of social action is "Responsibility," which all Christians recognize as the practical and non-sentimental meaning of the Pauline word "Charity." There is thus an individual rather than a collective focus even to Quaker social action, a democratic rather than a totalitarian approach to social reconstruction. A community of minds is achieved among Quakers by the normal processes of common opinion and natural leadership, not by bureaucratic directives. There would be widespread agreement among Quakers for universal hospitalization insurance, even if provided by the government, but not the same uniformity of opinion about nationalization of basic industries.

Quakers are thus, in the main, legitimate members of the fraternity of Evangelical Christians, possessing both the definable central ideas of classical Christianity, expressed with particular reference to the immediacy of personal experience (a marked Evangelical theme from St. Paul to John Wesley), and the common Christian view that the only Christian relationship to social problems is the practical one which seeks their solution. And even the solution turns out to be not bureaucratic but democratic, not purely material but also spiritual.

Because Mr. Cadbury is also a recognized New Testament Scholar, one of the collaborators on the *Revised Authorized New Testament,* it seemed appropriate to discuss with him briefly the significance of the role of the New Testament as Christianity's major primary source. Mr. Cadbury deplored the partiality of many New Testament interpreters, persons like Deissmann who trace a single idea like Platonism through the New Testament, as though that were its only element. It is possible to trace any particular strand of Christian thought through the New Testament, to be sure, but no one ought to be provincial enough to assume that he has thereby exhausted the contents of the Great Document. The so-called "Religion of Jesus," for example, as one of these particularist treatments, he said, is a transparent and thin distortion of a body of materials which actually transcend any such over-simplification. The so-called "Historical Approach" to the study of Christianity's First Anthology, he added, is another similar provincial distortion, believing it has captured the whole of a period when it has only captured its external remains, laboring under the delusion that it has caught the spirit of primitive

Christianity when it is debatable whether it has caught even its letter.

Seldom, for example, in Mr. Cadbury's experience, had anyone written on St. Paul as an actual human being, showing his many sidedness, in spite of the fact that he is the best-known personality in antiquity. Rather modern pseudo-scholars are always using, or abusing, St. Paul for the greater glory of their own partiality. St. Paul seems to transcend all particularist interpretations, as indeed the entire New Testament transcends its provincial expositors. One of the strongest elements, for example, in the New Testament is seldom mentioned, the obvious fact that the cluster of writers *assumed,* as something established beyond the necessity of proof, that Christ was the presence of God in man, even more than they deliberately declared it. "With this faith of early or classical Christianity modern secularists may violently disagree," he asserted, "but in no way is it possible to eliminate it from history."

JOHN DEWEY

Many young men pass through a period of radical thinking when they pride themselves on their sceptical frame of mind. They usually call themselves agnostics (it makes for less controversy, and it gives the impression, perhaps the presence, of intellectual humility), though a few go the whole distance and call themselves atheists. It is probably true, however, that young men are heretical (in the antique sense of overemphasis on partial truth) rather than purely radical, and maturity tends to restore an orthodox balance.

At one time in my own life, approximately from my twentieth to my thirtieth year, I was precisely such a young sceptic as I have described, except that I was thoroughly convinced in my atheism. During this period I looked upon John Dewey as a kind of patron saint. I often felt, and frequently said: "There is no God, and John Dewey is His Prophet." I read all of Dewey's books, with much the same attitude of mind as that with which

178

an old-fashioned fundamentalist approaches the sacred Bible. I believed in the literal and plenary inspiration of every word that proceeded out of the mouth of John Dewey.

Years passed, and atheism in religion and expediency in morals brought me to the edge of total breakdown — mental, moral, domestic, professional, and financial. I took the meaningless world view *seriously,* and based my conduct upon it. The result was, of course, disastrous, but even the fact of disaster did not, of itself, turn me from the swine-husks of the prodigal. Many additional influences were at work in my life, and inch by inch atheism and expediency gave ground to theism and morality. John Dewey himself, in his open-minded emphasis on enquiry rather than ontology, proved much later a major help. I do not, of course, wish to imply that John Dewey's instrumentalism, his relativistic pragmatism, uniformly produces immorality of conduct. It does not. Not infrequently, men reject, for moral or religious reasons, the immorality, and the religion, of the religious. Many a man — John Dewey himself, I think — had become (officially) an atheist *because* he was moral. That is, he reacted for moral reasons *against* all superstitious evasions of moral responsibility. I myself have known moralistic atheists. They were what the Russian, Dostoyevsky, called illegitimate children of Romanism, honest souls determined to have no part in a religion which for fifteen centuries has seemed to do violence to the free invitation of Christ's Gospel by uniting it, against its intrinsic nature, with the power and coercion of the state, which, in thorough-going totalitarian fashion, had occasionally subordinated every holy thing, including faith, to the unholy end of base earthly power. Men who are atheists for conscience sake, from Voltaire down, have made, on the whole, respectable citizens. There is no debate on the point. Nevertheless, in cold and disinterested fact, the interior logic of relativistic pragmatism, atheistic instrumentalism, and expediential utilitarianism, whether some actual atheist is or is not moral, atomizes every religious restraint on what Sorokin has called "the animal in man." The stoic atheist, I freely admit, is a better and more admirable man than the epicurean believer; the moral agnostic is more to be commended and emulated than the perverted religious man, to be sure. Yet, in all honesty, if there is such a thing as integrity in thought, the epicurean and the pervert are as legitimate as the stoic and the moralist — in an exclusively relative world. Where there is only an expedient right or wrong, wise personal taste and whim are the only final arbiters, and hard self-interest emerges from sentimental and nominal altruism.

Much water has gone under the bridge, therefore, since the break with my correct or incorrect understanding of John Dewey's dogmatic instrumentalism. Nevertheless I felt what one always feels toward a one-time hero, something akin to sentiment. As men travel to the Mecca of their choice, I journeyed all the way from Wisconsin to Manhattan's upper Fifth Avenue — solely to converse with John Dewey, a senior American voice of all the relativists, to ask him if he were still a typical nineteenth century cracker-barrel sceptic. Frankly I had entertained a secret hope that the late years, and the recent global contest between morality and expediency, might have mellowed the master in the direction of a meaningful world view. I confess myself disappointed in this secret hope, for my one-time Prophet proved to be still what he has always been. His metaphysics (the world has no ultimate purpose or meaning or objective; there is no Providence, no God!), his ethics (right is simply and only what will work in the relative context of this meaningless world!), and his conception of the chief end of man (not the fellowship of God, not moral and spiritual rectitude, but sensate well-being!), remain just where, and just what, they were. However, as *James,* in the New Testament, put it: "Show me your faith without your works, and I will show you my faith by my works; faith without works is dead."

He was amused at my statement that he had the unique distinction of being the articulate voice, apparently, of modern sensate man. He believed, he said, that he had some enemies. So wide a following, and so complete a discipleship, we agreed, might well make a man a bit sceptical and suspicious of his own skepticism.

Dewey's fundamental unbelief, which seems closer to bitterness toward religious immorality than metaphysical or structural atheism, issues from the old fact of suffering and hardship in the world, and the failure to perceive the significant evidence of man's heroic spirit. God has not strewn man's path with roses; there is a hardship or two. Ergo, God does not exist, or, if He does, is malignant, and worthy the nose-thumbing defiance of moral men — nineteenth century village skepticism, not seldom justifiable from the conduct of the "religious," pure and simple. Man's own courageous attack upon suffering and hardship is the over-looked and incontrovertible evidence that man's origin, destiny, and nature cannot be identical with the amoral forces he overcomes. The element most characteristically human in man, in John Dewey himself, is moral, free, responsible, and purposing, and beyond identification with the material, the necessitated, the non-responsible, and the non-purposing — indeed ultimately identifiable solely with a Cosmic Spirit, the Mind-Matter Unity, the Homeostasis or Equilibrium, of the Infinite Universe — a Reality not wholly unlike man, the bearer of his image — indeed, in Christian terms, man's Father in Heaven.

Dewey said: "If there is a God, it is high time He took a hand in human affairs" — to which I replied that he, Dewey, was in good company for the Psalmist shared the same idea, when he said: "How long, O Lord, how long?" Further, that Christians for nineteen hundred years had been sharing the same prayer in the words: "Thy Kingdom Come, Thy Will Be Done." In other words, men long for greater speed in evolution, and pray — "Get busy, Lord, get busy!"

Was there any hope for man's civilization? I asked. He smiled and replied: "Well, there's always faith and hope and love, and while we haven't much faith, and love is supposed to be greatest, we can't give up hope."

Mr. Dewey confessed that he could go along with the classic Christian statement that the chief end of man was to glorify God and enjoy Him forever, but only by re-defining the words "glorify God". He also acknowledged his appreciation of Micah's still-pertinent version of true religion, "to do justly, to love mercy, and to walk humbly with thy God", provided the words "with thy God" could be stricken out, and the sense of Divine (to him unreal) requirement abolished. Nonetheless, to do justly, to love mercy, and to walk humbly, were to him, and are to all the children of men, Free World necessities — indeed to organized religions and over- or under-organized governments as well. For a reasonable obedience to these ancient, and still modern, commands, what man, religion, or government would be excommunicated from Free World Fellowship?

He cited his extensive travels in China, and his feeling that the greatest obstacle to Christianity's advance throughout the world was its provinciality. He quoted the complaint of literate Chinese that Christian missionaries occasionally seemed to believe that their first task was to destroy Confucianism. Yet he agreed emphatically that Christianity was to be regarded, not as an alternative to other moral faiths, but as their fulfilment — even though the Word made flesh in Bethlehem was, in lesser part, meaning-less mythology to him. I was unable to convince him that mythology often represents a truth greater than, rather than less than, itself, a poetry at times truer than prose.

He wanted it clearly understood, he said, that in ethics he preferred long-range expediency rather than the short-range, near-sighted, partial and hedonistic variety. He felt that for all practical purposes long-range expediency and absolute morality were identical, which committed him to both.

At the close of our lengthy and genial interview, spiced with humor, I said: "Do you mind if I say, as I leave, 'God bless you, sir'?" He smiled, shook my hand with warm friendliness, and replied: "No, I don't mind. With a little re-definition I think I can go along with that."

I had hoped for a stronger bridge to intellectual communion, but perhaps no stronger need be found. He believed in long-range expediency as the meaning of morality, as the Absolute Demand both immanent and transcendent — the ethical Christian's understanding of God in Christ.

One thing was as clear as sunlight — he sought with all Free Minds the human better and the human more, which others have called "the Kingdom of Righteousness," and Christ Himself called, in this-worldly relations, "the Kingdom of Heaven" — not ghosts flitting like birds through the air, but the Good Spirit at work in all human lives, minds, and hearts, on Earth as in Heaven, in the Actual as in the Ideal.

One thing more, therefore, was clear. Let no one lose sight of it. The area of common humanity, of common humor, of common life and mind, the common love of freedom and trustworthy honor, *all* men may (and do, in fact) share together. In precisely this fellowship I was at ease and at home with John Dewey. Though our language differed, we were not in opposed armies to the end. I respect him as a father in moral faith, and love him as a fellow recipient of the good gift of life. With him I share the common hope that, faced with World Freedom and World Slavery alternatives, individual men, and their religious or secular governments, may, and will, choose the higher.

REINHOLD NIEBUHR

It was possible to spend only part of one afternoon, after years of reading and teaching his volumes, in the presumptuous attempt to vivisect the mind of Reinhold Niebuhr, for the writer was enroute to Europe and schedules were demanding. There was comfort in the hope that the future would find time for further Niebuhr reading.

Admittedly, no interviewer could hope in a brief compass to exhaust or, beyond generalities, to describe Niebuhr's original mind. Nevertheless it was possible to focus discussion around three or four disputed themes: If the anthropologist can reconstruct the whole life of primitive man from a single weapon, or an archaeologist a whole civilization from a fragment of pottery, it is not unthinkable that the broad outline of a great mentality can be sketched with some accuracy from a cluster of answers.

The first question sought to disclose Niebuhr's starting point: "What relation can be established, if any, between Thomism and Personalism?" I explained my view that the Roman philosophy, Thomism, was structural or architectural, with its three levels, science, philosophy, and revelation, but as incomplete by itself as an uninhabited three-story house. The Protestant philosophy, Personalism, on the other hand, with its emphasis upon the individual as the solitary focus of all knowledge and ethics, without the Thomist three-story house to live in, tended to solipsism at best and relativism at worst. Could not these dominant Christian philosophies, if held in wholesome tension, serve as mutual correctives?

With utmost grace, and with splendid attention to exact expression, Niebuhr explained his conviction that an unbridgeable chasm yawned between Thomism and Personalism. His Personalistic studies in graduate school had established Thomism's inescapable rationalism, its belief that man could think his way into all truth. In Personalism, as in the Niebuhr view, the individual could come to a knowledge of God only through the crisis of sin and repentance. More of the Divine, he felt, was revealed to the active conscience than to the keen intellect. In Thomist thought, on the other hand, it seemed, he said, that knowledge of the Divine could be grasped by the attentive mind with or without personal surrender to the Divine Will.

The second question concerned a bibliographical problem. "In what sequence do you recommend that your books be read?" He replied "I don't know that I would specially recommend one sequence above another. The most representative book would be *Beyond Tragedy*. My theological position is given, of course, in the various series of lectures. My ethical and political philosophy will be found in *The Children Of Light And The Children Of Darkness* and in *Christianity And Power Politics.*"

An issue very much in the thinking of leading Churchmen was presented in the third question: "What hope exists for a resurrection of Evangelical Protestantism, and what major steps must be taken to achieve this end?" As might have been anticipated, Niebuhr's answer outlined two prerequisites, neither of which could be safely neglected. The movement away from cultural obscurantism had to be quickened; the Evangelical Faith needed rescue from Literalism, Irrationalism, and Emotionalism. The Faith, though preserved in distorted or cramped form, had lost creative tension with the Present. Its anti-scientific emphasis had placed it out of touch with the modern mind, had thus rendered it inaccessible to the educated. The therapeutic battle against obscurantism's hardened arteries had to be waged with energy, or the heart of Evangelical Protestantism would fail.

The more important battle, however, for spiritual resurrection was against Relativism. In many minds the various liberal emphases had shattered the central Christian Ideas. Christianity could not win its dual war against secularism on the one hand and obscurantism on the other if confusion were substituted for its classical certainties — God, Christ, Original Sin, Grace, etc. If Christianity were nothing in Itself, then it was already dead. But if Something, then there was an undeniable cluster of definable Ideas at Its center. The greater battle of our time was against the loss of these Ideas, and for their vital recovery in Christian minds.

It was not necessary, he said, to surrender to the irrationalism of Rome (the worship of Mary, etc.) in order to be a Christian, for that irrationalism was hardly preferable to Protestant Literalism. To be a Christian, simply, involved the avoidance alike of the idolatry of the Church and the idolatry of the Bible. Christianity's central Ideas had to be preserved with equal vigor from intellectual nihilism and from intellectual anarchy.

In Niebuhr's opinion, the first battle was against external obscurantism, but the more important was the second, the battle against inward confusion, the obscurantism of bewilderment. No realistic service had been rendered by apologists, like Schleiermacher and Ritschl, he said, who sought to evade the ultimate questions by re-stating evolution in religious terminology, and were thus committed neither to meaning nor to non-meaning as ultimately true. The collected absence of a point of view, which often passed for cultural breadth, was powerless as a propagandist for any Christianity worth having. Insofar as essential Christian theology was shattered in contemporary Protestantism, Protestantism itself was both inwardly and socially sterile. This way lay extinction, not resurrection.

The admirable Ecumenical movement, should it abandon the Christian centralities, would contribute only to a distinctionless merger, an essentially valueless syncretism.

The last question moved from philosophy and faith to the mundane world of political economy. "To what extent can an individual who is right-wing theologically be left-wing politically?" Niebuhr asserted at once that, so far as he was concerned, the two positions were necessarily united. Clearly, the implication of classical Christianity — of the Idea of Original Sin, for example — was that power could corrupt any class of men. Selfishness, from which even good people were by no means exempt, made inadvisable the concentration of government in any class, however enlightened. Power could not be wielded by a class for that class, whether of saints or sinners, of kings, or parliaments, or proletariats, without loss to all disinherited internal minorities. "To what extent," I asked, "can a shallow externalism be avoided in the endeavor to solve all our problems by legislation?" Niebuhr emphasized that the legislative solution to a social problem was only one, and if pursued alone a very superficial one. However, on the analogy of St. Paul, as illness in one part of the body produced discomfort in all, so one solution to a social problem contributed to all. In any case, some part of the endeavor to restrain human selfishness had to be external, for men were forced to set up obstacles to the self-aggrandizement of the few at the expense of the many. Wherever greed entrenched itself in predatory minorities — whether economic royalists, labor dictators, or Russian Communists — the common interest required a united resistance. All government was in part external, if not primarily so, and, if it were not to be abandoned altogether, it would have to be made an instrument for the practical restraint of Original Sin.

In American thinking the concept of Freedom tended to be divorced from the equally important concept of Community. Totalitarians exalted a Community of Coercion and excluded Freedom, but Americans tended toward the complete denial of Community — surely as flagrant a departure from well-being. In England and Sweden, whence Niebuhr had but recently returned to the United

States, literate opinion regarded America as virtually at the extreme of anarchy. European leaders did not feel that they had given up Freedom where, for example, they had adopted universal hospital insurance or nationalized the mines. The American political right-wing made a metaphysics of Free Enterprise. Freedom, set up as an Idol, was worshipped at the costly price of human suffering. The Worship of Private Property was as unsatisfying a substitute for the worship of the True God as State-worship had ever been. Original Sin was as deadly under the institutions of Free Enterprise as in any totalitarian tyranny. The weak were to be protected from the strong, the few from the many, minorities from majorities — and the reverse. The Community was obligated therefore to set up a regime of law, externally enforced, as well as inwardly approved.

Niebuhr's paradoxical position, uniting right-wing theology with left-wing politics, makes him singularly stimulating to contemporary leaders. In their judgments of him his opponents quickly classify themselves. Literalists regard him as too radical, and Liberals regard him as too conservative. One Relativist of the economic royalist class described Niebuhr to me as a writer "gifted with an electric brilliance of style, but too shallow;" a Liberal of the Socialist class said: "Niebuhr is stimulating, but he's not left-wing enough; he's not even a Socialist." As G. K. Chesterton once suggested, a position equally damned from opposite extremes, obviously occupying the middle of the road, must be the true one.

CONCLUSION

Many Faces, One Freedom and Faithfulness in Fellowship:
Christianity Is Thinkable

A common idea among thinking Christians is the relevance of Ecumenical Christianity to the development of World Democracy. As Toynbee has put it, a united Christianity created Europe; Christian dis-unity produced Nationalism; only Christianity, truly united, can create One World. The Catastrophe of our time, not yet ended, in Berdiaeff's words, may arouse Central Christianity from lethargy. The Giant awakened can restore European unity once given and once lost. Without spiritual and moral unity, political unity can come only to grief. What, therefore, is, or was, Christianity? Christianity, a living Fellowship across the centuries, as understood by its best qualified spokesmen, is Thinkable and, within certain limits, Definable. It is not a Fog, not a collected Absence of Beliefs. At its center, in one age as in another, always presented in the language of a particular time and place, there has been, and today continues to be, an Identifiable Cluster of Ideas.

I began a series of interviews with major modern writers in many European countries with the belief that a basic Christian mentality exists in diverse forms in contemporary Christendom. This belief was abundantly justified by the actual conversations. It is not possible to summarize in a few conclusions all that was said of significance on the Content of Christianity. Two ideas, however, shared in common by most of the men interviewed, are crystal clear. Objectively, Christianity is to be recognized, in the terms of the World Council of Churches, as "faith in Christ as God and Saviour," a true and final invitation to mankind. An initial faith in a human yet Divine Christ is the door of entrance to the Christian Cathedral.

Within that Edifice all things are reevaluated. Faith in Christ underemphasizes neither God the Father nor God the Holy Spirit. It includes rather than excludes a thorough understanding of Man and the State, of personal and corporate Discipleship. Without apology, Christianity is identifiable with specific belief in the Deity and the Humanity of Christ. As Toynbee has put it in his *Study of History,* Christ is "not the Deputy of God but Himself God, not an underling but the King of the Kingdom of Heaven." Creedally, objectively, Christianity forever centers around this defining, and, if you like, limiting Conviction.

Subjectively, Christianity exists only where men today are inwardly, seriously committed to seek and obey the Will of God, to rejoice in His Love, to share the Companionship of the Holy Spirit, to enthrone Christ in the mind, the strength, the heart, and the soul, and, in His Name, to accept realistic responsibility for the neighbor near and far. All the objective, or creedal Christianity, in the world, without subjective Christianity, is dead. All the subjective Christianity in the world, without objective Christianity, is, or will shortly become, Solipsism or Anarchy, and therefore equally sterile. Objective Christianity can always produce new life, for men may at any time take inwardly and seriously what is objectively clear. Subjectivity alone has an inevitable fissiparous drive.

Christianity Is Transmissible

The Church itself, however administered, is both the Medium of Christian Fellowship, and the Divine/Human Device of Evangelism. This idea, in varied form, emerged with emphasis from every interview. Christianity is not merely a Doctrine and a Discipline; it is also an Impact upon total societies and individual souls. Karl Barth believed the entire Christian Community, that is, the Church and the Society it creates and regenerates (in our case European and American Civilization) is the Divine method of Evangelism. Arnold J. Toynbee stressed the individual Christian, obedient in will and faith and love, as the primary technique of Christian assault upon secularism. Clearly, the two accents are two aspects of one thing, for the individual Christian is the Church in miniature; the Church is the Company of Pilgrims; and the Christian Society is a tension, on T. S. Eliot's terms, between the Church and the Civilization it helps to form.

If the Christian Civilization, the Church, and the Christian are the effective techniques of Evangelism, Kraemer's emphasis upon the re-spiritualization of the Church through prayer and faith is a significant necessity. Maritain's insistence upon the recovery of personal mysticism, and an accompanying resurrection of intellectual vitality, simply underscores the necessity of a Christianity alert in Church and Disciple. Emil Brunner's accent upon "a live theology," like Maritain's insistence upon an intellectual revival, stresses Christian content as essential to Christian transmission. T. S. Eliot's belief that a theological renaissance is desperately needed in university education is identical. A common cry for greater attention to the World Council, as a means of clarifying Christian thought and awakening a consciousness of Christian unity, constitutes a plea for a spiritually and intellectually re-vitalized Church — hence, for spiritually and intellectually alert Christians. There is One Church of Christ, whether Roman or Catholic or both in Parliament, one Tree with Many Branches. Effective Evangelism requires a deepened consciousness of Unity, alike in faith and action. The Ecumenical Church is itself a major device of Evangelism, of Telefinalism — if you like, in Human Evolution.

This is the basic view of the transmissibility of Christianity common to most of the thinkers interviewed: the Church, to be an instrument of the Holy Spirit, has to make up its mind about Central Christianity, and renew the Christian message in a troubled world.

Christianity Is Practical

Contrary to the nineteenth century cry that Christianity is exclusively otherworldly, every man interviewed stressed three ideas: 1) Christianity is not primarily a means to a political end; it is a Process by which the endlessly creative God re-endows souls with creativity; 2) Christianity demands group solutions to group problems; and 3) Christianity demands that the individual be considered not as a means but an end.

Christianity was universally believed to furnish no specific planks for political platforms; it was rather the Critic of all platforms. However, the majority of Continental thinkers believed that social planning to guarantee the fair distribution of limited resources was an essential expression of Christian responsibility. No person interviewed, except Hanus Lomsky, favored Marxian materialism; none favored class antagonism. All except one believed that social responsibility could only become effective under a sense of Divine Compulsion. Thinkers in England stressed spiritual freedom as a necessity which must be maintained alongside social planning. Socialism in England was sometimes regarded as doctrinaire rather than realistic; yet everywhere attention to community necessity was acknowledged as a basic Christian requirement.

A common feature of continental Christianity was the political conservatism of Theological Relativists and the political radicalism of Theological Conservatives.

Nationalization of basic industries, universal hospital insurance, high labor standards, civic-minded action to improve the lot of the poor — these were frequently regarded as Christian essentials, particularly in view of post-war shortages.

Christianity demanded a balance, a paradox, in the Political world — group action for the solution of group problems, with the mobilization of the human best, and, at the same time, the protection of minorities and the rights of individuals. Community necessity and spiritual freedom — these two concepts were uniformly stressed as the basic concerns of Christian stewardship in the here and now.

Christianity was both supersensory and sensory, seeking first God and His Fellowship from which might flow endless re-birth, but seeking also a true stewardship in material things. Maritain felt that Protestant Christianity, unlike Romanism, has had no doctrine of the State. Protestantism, he said, dismissed the State from the Church, then criticized the State for becoming secular. Gilson believed Christianity was obligated to make Christ's will prevail upon earth, in the total political world, as in heaven. Whatever past Protestantism may have believed, present Protestantism, including sacred personal freedom in its understanding of the economic and religious will of God, it is clear, is of one mind with Gilson.

TELOS

The other day, a friend asked, "If one is convinced he should not vote for the *parliamentary* meeting of World Council of Churches and Rome, what should one vote for?"

The answer is as simple and honest as a child: "He should vote for the union of Moscow and Rome — the wedding, in economic, ecclesiastical, political, and religious slavery, of materialist and spiritualist ecumenicity, if only as a potent, and potential, though short term, intermediate necessity."

You ask, "Is such a meeting possible?" I suggest, "If the answer is not 'No!,' man is indeed not basically rational, the unoriginal item called 'Original Sin' is the permanently hopeless fact of human nature."

In other words: a third thing, as well as Communism and Romanism, is world-minded; it receives less publicity, but is the deeper force in *all* humankind, the desire and the demand for World Community, not ending but beginning with United Nations Organization and Council of Churches.

It takes *more* courage, more Godlikeness, to admit you were wrong, than to insist that you were right. How else Evolution, the Education of the human race?

Put differently, perhaps no man was, or is, *completely* honest, but, quite possibly, one man, the God/man, Christ. Who is the Spirit of Truth, the Spirit of Honesty, of Holy Communion, Holy Community, but the Holy Spirit?

In whom is honesty, another word for what the Psychiatrists call "unemotional empathy," required, sought, and expected, but mankind?

If you will forgive a personal word: I have learned a lot from my remarkable wife, but also from our two daughters, their husbands and families, and our remarkable son: I am a bit jealous of him — he has crossed the Atlantic 14 times, I only 12; he has experienced 4 years of private school in England, where quality more than quantity is stressed, plus 4 years of private school in America — 8,000 miles, twice a year, in Columbus Boychoir School concerts about the nation, 2 years, a month each, of 4 or 5 shows a day in Radio City Music Hall, Manhattan. At 14 years of age, for who knows what reasons, he had decided to be a minister, like his father and grandfather before him, a clergyman, denomination as yet unspecified. Should one try to talk him out of it?

In short, why did Christ love the children, at times, more than their diversely and strictly schooled parents? Perhaps because humility, teachableness, is another word for honesty, quite possibly more common than you think.

Little folks, dear friends, seem, perhaps are, less bound by austere adult prejudice (of race, class, or creed), not seldom a bit closer than Doctors of Philosophy, Parsons, and Priests to God the Father of all.

Did not Jesus, who according to Matthew and Luke could trace His human ancestry through many, many generations of Jews, invite His first disciples, who were Jews, and multiplied millions of non-Jewish disciples since — all more Catholic than Sectarian, whether Jewish or Greek or Roman or Protestant — to say, and say again, to His Father: "Our Father, who art in Heaven, hallowed be Thy Name; Thy Kingdom come; Thy Will be done, on Earth as it is in Heaven. Give us this day our daily bread, and forgive us our trespasses, as we forgive them that trespass against us. Lead us not into temptation, but deliver us from evil. For Thine is the Kingdom, and the Power, and the Glory forever. Amen."

DATE DUE
